DATE DUE			
Dec 16 77			

ASPECTS OF GREEK AND ROMAN LIFE

General Editor: H. H. Scullard

★ ★ ★

ARMS AND ARMOUR OF THE GREEKS

A. M. Snodgrass

ARMS AND ARMOUR OF THE GREEKS

A. M. Snodgrass

CORNELL UNIVERSITY PRESS
ITHACA, NEW YORK

399
SɴSa
99724
Jan. 1977

CORNELL UNIVERSITY PRESS

First published 1967
Second printing 1976

International Standard Book Number 0-8014-0399-5
Library of Congress Catalog Card Number 67-20632
Printed in the United States of America

CONTENTS

LIST OF ILLUSTRATIONS

INTRODUCTION

ARMS AND ARMOUR have formed the subject of many large and scholarly books, but these have in the main been restricted to the Middle Ages, being inspired by the great collection of medieval armour in the museums and great houses of Europe, and by the sense of national heritage associated with them. The purpose of the present work is rather different. For one thing, the state of the evidence for Greek arms and armour is so fragmentary, and its meaning at times so ambiguous, that no book has, to my knowledge, been attempted on the whole of this subject before. In repairing this omission, the first duty is perhaps to the student of classical history and literature; I hope that this work will at least make clear to him what a thing of shreds and patches our knowledge of this field still is. In particular, the imbalance which will be detected here in the treatment of the various periods of Greek history is largely a result of the uneven quality of our evidence; a reading of Chapter V, for instance, will show that it is little more than an attempt to synthesize the views that other writers have based on a bare framework of ancient sources.

A more general and widespread interest could perhaps be served if the subject could be set against its historical background. It may be wondered whether arms and armour have a place in history at all; especially in Greek history, where the course of most military events is so ill-documented as to provide a perennial field for controversy. Again, the Greeks were not, in the Classical period at least, a bellicose people; the horrors of war were clearly as much a commonplace to them as its glories, and not only amongst thinking men. Nor was their country particularly rich, either in population or in the raw materials of war. Given these facts, it is remarkable that the Greeks came to excel as often as they did in war. The traditional explanation has been to attribute this, along with many other aspects of the 'Greek miracle', to the unique national qualities of the people. While this claim has still some truth, the time has long since come to look beyond it. We shall never know quite how Marathon was won, but we can be fairly certain that valour alone would not have won it, nor even perhaps the combination of courage with the somewhat rudimentary tactical skills for which the style of Greek warfare at that time gave scope. The superiority of Greek equipment must have been an important factor here and elsewhere, and at times perhaps a decisive one. There are other influences, in the social and political fields, which are attributable to Greek armour and weapons, as is the case with some more primitive peoples; but it is their influence on military events, some of them out-standingly important, which perhaps gives them most significance.

This claim must not be exaggerated. We cannot attribute many Greek feats of arms to an individual weapon or piece of equip-ment, in the way in which we often can in more recent history. But underlying the sometimes naïve or confused accounts of battles by ancient authors, especially those concerned with the Persian Wars of the fifth and fourth centuries, is a conviction that the accepted 'inferiority' of the barbarian extended to the sphere of weapons and armour, and that this had much to do with the Greek successes. We shall ask in due course how well-grounded this conviction was.

One of the first tasks, however, must be to examine the different types of evidence available to us in studying a subject of this nature. In a literate society, we might expect written texts to form the prime source of information, but this is not so in Greece, at least until the very latest years of Greek indepen-dence. In any case, it is not until well on in our period that Greece becomes anything approaching a fully literate society. Before then, we have to consider the Mycenaean period, from which only the clay tablets and other objects inscribed in the Linear B script survive, and the succeeding Dark Age, in which to all appearances illiteracy was complete. Of the Linear B tablets, it must be said at once that our understanding of them is partial and disputed; but we can stay on firmer ground by concentrating our attention on the ideograms, some of them thumb-nail sketches of pieces of armour and other objects, which often appear on them.

From the late eighth century BC on, we can begin to draw on genuine literary sources for warfare and arms, although for some three hundred years these remain exclusively poetic. This in itself must impair their value as evidence; the poet, in Dr Johnson's words, 'does not number the streaks of the tulip'. To this general difficulty we must add another special factor: the Homeric poems, the earliest and greatest of these poetical sources, have as their setting a much older period. In no single passage of the *Iliad* or *Odyssey* can we be certain whether the poet is describing, accurately or otherwise, the arms and practices of that earlier period or those of his own day—except by reference to external evidence, principally from archaeology. The poems can thus hardly be used to fill gaps in our archaeological knowledge.

With the fifth century comes the rise of Greek prose literature: in particular the histories of the great struggle against the Persians in the first part of that century, and of the internal and external wars of Greece towards and after its end. Such contemporary or near-contemporary accounts have an unparalleled value for posterity, but in their own nature they are unlikely to be very informative about the details of Greek arms and equipment, which were already familiar to their readers. There also survive some Greek military manuals of a practical nature; the best of these, such as Xenophon's *On Horsemanship*, may contain some useful information; but of the most serious and thorough works, like those of Aeneas Tacticus in the fourth century BC and of Hero of Alexandria and Philo of Byzantium in the third, the surviving parts are concerned with siege-warfare and so fall outside the scope of this book.

These then are the limitations of our literary evidence. Curiously enough, some of them also apply to our second main source, the field of artistic representations. In Greek archaeology, this means predominantly vase-paintings. As a source for Greek arms and armour, these perhaps occupy the same position as do

monumental brasses for medieval chivalry. There is valuable illus-
trative material also to be found in Greek sculpture, particularly
relief-sculpture, and on metal relief-work and occasionally gems
and coins. But the artists in all these media very often chose their
subject-matter from saga and myth; as a rule, this did not prevent
them from showing the arms and equipment of their own day
but on occasions the context led them, as it sometimes led their
contemporaries the poets, to introduce 'heroic property' into their
pictures. Sometimes these elements took the form of accurate
portrayals of the equipment of bygone days, but more often the
portrayals were distorted, and occasionally they were drawn from
the field of pure imagination, as was the aegis of Athena. To
distinguish such elements from the observed, real-life properties
of contemporary warfare is difficult, and is only made possible
by the presence of our third main class of evidence: the actual
specimens of armour and weapons found by excavation.

Here of course we are on much firmer ground. A sword or a
metal helmet is solid and unambiguous evidence in itself, provided
that we can recognize and, scarcely less important, approximately
date it. This second condition cannot always be satisfied; arms
and armour are not often datable in themselves, on internal
evidence. We need the help of other materials, chiefly pottery,
which are normally associated with them in a grave or deposit;
and such associations have not always been observed. The science
of excavation is still a comparatively young one, and even since
its birth the older practice of mere treasure-hunting has by no
means died out. Armour in particular, perhaps in its nature, has
more often been the prize of the looter than of the scientific
archaeologist; and the result is that a high proportion of the
finds in museums and other collections are simply recorded as
having been found in a certain site or district, without further
details; sometimes even the provenance is unknown. To this
unhappy rule there are exceptions and, in the Greek field, one
outstanding one: in the German excavations at Olympia an
unparalleled collection of arms and armour, much of it in fine
condition, has come to light year by year. It is being systematically
published, and a representative selection is exhibited in Olympia

Museum. Already in the second century AD people were digging up arms at Olympia (Pausanias V, 20, 8). Other important collections in Greece are in the National Museum and Kerameikos Museum, Athens; and in the museums of Heraklion, Delphi and Argos. The collections outside Greece were mainly formed in earlier days, and so are less well documented. We may mention especially those in the former Staatliche Museen, Berlin and in Karlsruhe; in the Louvre and the Bibliothèque Nationale, Paris; in Naples Museum; in the British Museum, the Ashmolean Museum (Oxford) and the Fitzwilliam Museum (Cambridge); and, on the other side of the Atlantic, those of the Metropolitan Museum, New York and the City Art Museum, St. Louis, although I cannot speak of these at first hand. It goes without saying that virtually all the surviving armour and weapons of ancient times are made of metal or other durable materials. But we should remember that, at many periods, perishable materials like wood and leather were also widely used, so that this limitation on our evidence could easily lead to a distorted picture.

Such are the main classes of evidence at our disposal. Each has its own defects, which the others can do something to redeem. The writer, and especially the poet, cannot be expected to give a fully satisfactory description of a mundane object like a shield or spear, while the artist, especially in the inhibiting medium of vase-painting, may not have the space or the technique to represent it; but in both cases our task will be easier if we have actual examples to compare with their portrayals. Conversely, a piece of equipment in itself may be incomplete, unrecognizable or of uncertain use, and in this case literary or artistic evidence may provide the necessary clue. It is only by combining all the different strands that we can hope to weave a coherent picture of the development of arms and armour in Greece.

CHAPTER I

THE MYCENAEANS

MYCENAEAN ARMS and armour have attracted increasing attention in recent years. Several groups of the contemporary Linear B tablets record military equipment; the Homeric *Iliad* is a later picture, whether accurate or otherwise, of the late Mycenaean world at war; and, generally, the Mycenaeans appear to have been a fairly warlike people. Again, much of the fundamental and direct evidence is only now coming to light; for instance, almost all of the metal armour known from the Mycenaean world has been found or identified since 1950. Besides this, we have numerous weapons, a handful of vase-paintings, a few other representations and the enigmatic evidence of the Linear B tablets. We should bear in mind that much of this evidence may refer to equipment which was perishable and cannot therefore be matched among the extant finds, such as shields of ox-hide and corslets or jerkins of leather or textile material.

Three main phases in the development of Mycenaean armament seem to emerge from this body of evidence. The first belongs largely to the sixteenth century BC, and is mainly represented by the rich finds from the two groups of Shaft-graves excavated at Mycenae itself. The second corresponds very roughly with the second half of the fifteenth and the first half of the fourteenth centuries, and the evidence comes not only from mainland Greece, but from graves in the Dodecanese and the vicinity of the palace of Knossos in Crete, a centre which many believe to have fallen under Mycenaean control at this time; not to mention the many Linear B tablets found in the palace itself. The third phase belongs to the last flowering of Mycenaean power in the Aegean area, extending from the thirteenth century to the early twelfth, and again includes Linear B tablets, this time dating from around 1200 BC. These phases are separated by intervals, of which our knowledge is even slighter than usual. It would be wrong to demarcate the phases too sharply, but there seem to have been fundamental differences between them in the equipment and practices of warfare. All three phases lie within the Aegean Late Bronze Age, and the offensive weapons are almost exclusively of bronze.

THE SHAFT-GRAVE PERIOD

The period of the Shaft-graves, although the earliest, is well-documented within narrow social and geographical limits.[1] The princes buried at Mycenae were apparently as warlike as they were rich; both the quantity and, in some cases, the quality of the equipment interred with them far exceeded the needs of real life. For instance, in Shaft-grave V, Schliemann, the excavator, estimated that at least ninety swords in all had accompanied the three men buried there. Some of the weapons were so embellished with inlay-work and with attachments of gold, ivory and other materials that they can hardly have been meant for everyday use. There was no real armour in the graves; instead we have frail objects in beaten gold or silver which must stand for real-life equipment in humbler, probably non-metallic materials. The picture is extended by the representations, in which the two favourite subjects are those which were to predominate throughout Mycenaean art, war and the chase; they are our best evidence for the defensive armour of the period.

But it is on the offensive weapons, and especially the swords, that the limelight falls. The invention of the true sword was a fateful step in history; at this date it was still almost a novelty. The long rapier, which was the commonest type in the Shaft-graves, was not Mycenaean in origin, but had been developed by the Minoan bronzesmiths of Crete, as an improvement on the less impressive weapons used by the peoples of the Near East.[2] It is a huge weapon—many of the extant examples exceed three feet in length, without the elaborate hilt-attachments with which they were originally fitted—but this in itself reduced its practical value. A heavy blow on the edge of the sword, if it did not shatter the slender blade, was likely to snap the even thinner tang, so that hilt and blade parted company. In many cases the swords have been found with their tangs broken in this way, probably during use. Strictly these are thrusting-weapons, and their designed use must have been largely limited to the fencing duels, between single champions, which we see represented on some signet-rings of the period.

Side by side with these giant rapiers in the Shaft-graves there were found, in much smaller quantity, examples of a new and much more serviceable type of sword.[3] This, in contrast, is of only medium length, and seems to have been developed by the Mycenaeans themselves. It shows several advances on the older type of sword, and one of them is crucial—the enlargement of the tang into a genuine hilt, with flanges along each side. In general it was a less clumsy and more versatile weapon than the first type of sword, and its flatter blade may possibly have allowed it to be used for cutting strokes.

The swords, and especially those of the second type, are re-produced on a smaller scale as daggers; there are also short swords or choppers with one cutting edge, probably for house-hold use.[4] The dagger, too, has always been an implement at least as much for domestic as for warlike use, and it will not figure largely in this book. Its chief importance is in the fact that it often served as a prototype for experiments which, if successful, were later translated into full-length swords. As a practical offensive weapon, it is eclipsed by the spear and the bow.

Spearheads are only found in the Shaft-graves in small numbers. This could mean that the spear was less esteemed as a weapon or, on the contrary, that it was so indispensable that only a bare minimum of one or two per man could be spared for inter-ment. Since the spear is as often shown in contemporary battle-scenes as the sword, and is almost universal in hunting-scenes, we may suspect that the second alternative is nearer to the truth. The biggest spearheads found in the graves are massive weapons, nearly two feet in length, with a leaf-shaped blade and a long protruding socket into which the wooden shaft fitted. This shaft, to balance the head, must have been of great length; in one representation, the lion-hunt inlaid on a dagger-blade, the spears shown, if they are to scale, must be at least ten feet in over-all length.[5] These great weapons, like the largest swords, were adopted from the Minoans of Crete, There could be no question of throwing a spear of this size, but some much smaller heads, one as little as six inches long, were found in the graves, and these may well have belonged to javelins.[6] In later Mycenaean hunting-scenes and, very rarely, in war, we see men carrying two spears each, which are presumably to be thrown; sometimes the huntsman's quarry is shown pierced by a javelin.[7] *Pl. 2*

If the spear has an ambiguous status, as a weapon both of war and of the chase, the bow has it to a far more marked degree. The Greeks of later days did not think highly of the bow for military use, and scholars have tended to transfer this attitude to an earlier period, and to dismiss the evidence of Mycenaean archery as being exclusively concerned with hunting. This view is probably mistaken. Ancient bows, being of perishable material, have survived only in exceptional circumstances, such as interment in the sealed tombs of Egypt, but in the Shaft-graves many arrowheads of flint and some of obsidian, as well as bronze ones were found.[8] The flint examples in particular are miniature masterpieces, carefully shaped, almost indestructible and with their edges sharpened to a fineness which metal could not then rival. Flint is scarce in Greece and it has been suggested that these arrowheads were imported from Egypt; even for obsidian the Mycenaeans had to go as far as Melos in the Cyclades. All this argues an interest in archery perhaps too intensive to be explained in terms of sport or food-gathering. The common type of bronze arrowhead clearly imitates the flint and obsidian shapes: all three forms were nearly flat, and were used in the same way, being inserted into a slot in the tip of the arrow-shaft. We have only a few glimpses of the bow which was used with these arrows;[9] in Mycenaean representations it is almost always of the plain European type, the 'self' bow made from a single stave of wood. By the next century, as we shall see, there is better evidence that the Mycenaeans were using this same type of bow and arrowhead for warfare. In one grave occurred examples of the 'arrow-shaft-polisher', a special kind of whetstone probably used for this purpose.[10] It is very common in northern Europe, and its appearance here is one of the first signs of communication between Mycenae and its European hinterland.

The warrior of the Shaft-grave era could thus take the field with a powerful armoury of weapons of attack. For his defensive armour we have far less direct evidence. The very thin breast-plates of gold foil found on three of the male bodies in the group of graves excavated by Schliemann, were clearly designed for decorative and perhaps ceremonial use.[11] They need not imply that the dead princes wore metal breastplates in battle in their lifetime, and indeed the parallel case of the silver miniature shield (p. 20) makes this even less likely. A tiny fragment of linen, fourteen layers thick, was found in Shaft-grave V and may be part of a linen corslet. With the gold breastplates one may tentatively compare the rather commoner gold bands, bent into a circle and with an arm projecting downwards, which have usually been identified as a kind of suspender for leggings; but their fragility and precious material again show that they were not for everyday use.[12] In Shaft-grave IV appeared the only metal objects which can plausibly be connected with genuine armour for use in battle: a group of more than forty small bronze discs, perforated for attachment to some sort of backing, for a helmet or other armour.[13]

For the helmet, however, we have much better evidence in a different material. A number of Mycenaean representations, some of them quite detailed, show helmets composed of several horizontal bands of small, roughly crescent-shaped objects packed closely together, those of each band facing alternate ways. At the end of the last century, the German scholar Wolfgang Reichel saw that these curved pieces were meant to represent thin plates specially cut from the tusks of a wild boar, such as had been found in some quantity on Mycenaean sites.[14] These plates were attached to a cap of some softer material, now perished; the helmet, though laborious to make, would have been stout enough. It must also have been a mark of hunting prowess: some thirty or forty boars would have to be killed to furnish a set of tusks for each helmet. But the most remarkable thing about this helmet is that an example is accurately described in Book X of the Homeric *Iliad*, which reached its final form at least eight hundred years after the Shaft-grave era:

'And on his head he placed a helmet made of hide; on the inside it was stoutly made with many taut thongs; outside, the white tusks of a boar with gleaming teeth, closely arrayed, facing alternate ways, were well and cleverly set; in between a cap of felt was fitted' (lines 261-5).

Since Reichel explained this passage, the boars' tusk helmet has been found to have a pedigree reaching back into the Middle Bronze Age in Greece. It is a distinctively European type, being rare in Minoan Crete, and it is worth noting that there was a tradition for the use of boars' tusks for body-protection in other parts of Europe. *Pl. 8*

The most remarkable item in the panoply of the Shaft-grave warrior was his shield. There are two types of shield represented on the monuments of this period, and both are very large— four feet or more in height, if the scale of the representations can be trusted.[15] They can only have been made of ox-hide, and indeed are sometimes shown dappled in black and white, but there are also occasional hints of metal reinforcement. The commoner of the two varieties is in the shape of a rough figure-of-eight when seen from the back or front; in profile it is seen to be of strongly convex form, with a 'waist', slightly pinched in, rather less than half way down. This explains its construction, which must have been from a hide cut to roughly oval shape and then braced on a long, slightly curved vertical stave; a short cross-piece, also convex, drew the sides slightly inwards at the point where it reached them. Sometimes the lateral curve was so pronounced that a large vertical fold was formed down the middle. Less common and slightly smaller is the plain 'tower' shield, which had straight rims at the sides but an upward curve in the top edge and, again, a strong lateral convexity which shows in profile views. Both shields formed a kind of mobile embrasure, which gave some protection to the warrior's sides as well as his front. But they must have been extremely unwieldy; there is no sign that they had handles, and they seem to have been held and manoeuvred solely by means of a strap which passed over the left shoulder, behind the neck and under the right arm-pit. When desired, they could simply be thrown over the left shoulder and left to hang down the back. To the many pictures of these shields we may now add a large silver model of the 'figure-of-eight' type, found in Shaft-grave IV but only recognized and reconstructed eighty years later.[16] Here again, as with the boars' tusk helmet, it is remarkable that body-shields of this size are occasionally mentioned or implied in the *Iliad*; in particular, the shield 'like a tower' which Ajax regularly uses is surely to be identified with this second type of body-shield. So, too, when Hector's shield, slung over his back, bumps against his neck and ankles as he runs along (VI, 118), and when Periphetes of Mycenae trips over backwards on the rim of his shield (XV, 645), we may detect survivals of this type. The body-shield, at least that of figure-of-eight shape, occurs very early in Minoan Crete and was probably acquired at a later date by the Mycenaeans from that source. *Pl. 2*

The kings of Mycenae had the use of one other war arm, new to Europe and potentially of great importance, the chariot. Some of the tombstones which stood over the Shaft-graves are carved in low relief, and three of them show a warrior—presumably the dead man—riding in a chariot. This vehicle, like the bow and spear, could be used for hunting as well as warfare, and is many times portrayed in scenes of the chase. But the appearance of chariots in Greece for either purpose is always puzzling; the terrain is usually too rough to allow them to operate except on a made track, which would severely inhibit their use. They probably served purposes of prestige as much as anything, and we need not accept too literally the scenes on these gravestones, which are normally taken to represent the warrior running down his enemies.[17] *Pl. 1*

THE PALACE PERIOD

The developments in Mycenaean armour during the following centuries were no doubt very gradual, but we can nevertheless identify a distinct second phase, datable between the rough limits of 1450 and 1350 BC. It partly coincides with the production of the huge painted jars which form the 'Palace Style' of pottery, and we may perhaps refer to this as the Palace period. The evidence is now much more broadly based. Although we still depend largely on tombs, we are no longer confined to those of a single royal dynasty. The graves now belong to what seems to be a class of warrior aristocrats, serving the royal palaces; they are extended geographically over several areas of the Greek mainland and islands. To the end of this period belong many (probably almost all) of the baked clay tablets excavated in and near the palace at Knossos by Sir Arthur Evans; they include over two hundred texts and fragments which, as their accompanying ideograms alone would show, refer to armour and weapons. The date suggested by the most recent authorities for the fall of the palace is in the region of 1375–1350 BC.[18] Warrior graves, Palace Style pottery and Linear B tablets are all among the features which distinguish Knossos from most other Cretan sites in the period just before its fall, and which have led most scholars to the opinion that Knossos had become a dependency of the Mycenaean mainland. The innovations which distinguish this Palace period from the era of the Shaft-graves are, in our field, mostly in the form of improvements and modifications of existing arms. But there is one important and fundamental change—the mastery of the production of plate armour by Mycenaean bronzesmiths. Now, probably for the first time in European history, begin to appear bronze body-armour and, perhaps a little later, bronze helmets: a result, perhaps, of the fusion of Minoan skills with Mycenaean military ambitions.

In weapons, many of the changes simply arise from the weaknesses of the Shaft-grave prototypes. Thus the earliest swords, for all their great size and imposing appearance, had structural weaknesses, mainly in the hilting. The two new types now developed, the 'horned' and the 'cruciform' sword, were both designed to cure this.[19] The horned sword takes its name from the long, slim hilt with its two horn-like projections of bronze, forming the handguard. Possibly these swords could be used for a cutting stroke; certainly they were admired and imitated by foreign peoples extending from Palestine to the Danube. The cruciform sword is a more modest cousin of the horned type, and is even commoner. It too has a 'one-piece' construction, with flanges on the hilt, but its hand-guard projections are rounded and at right angles to the blade, giving the sword its name; it is generally shorter than the horned sword. It seems to have developed from an older dagger of Minoan origin, which had shoulders of much the same shape, and may thus have been a Cretan type—one of the last in the field of warfare that the Mycenaeans adopted. To judge from the graves, a single sword was now sometimes considered enough for each warrior; the only common combination is one long (usually horned) and one short sword; these are likely to have been used for different kinds of combat rather than simultaneously, one in each hand, in the manner of later sword-play. *Pls. 3, 4*

At this point the first relevant group of Linear B tablets, the twenty-two 'Sword' tablets found in the domestic wing of the palace at Knossos, should be mentioned. The ideograms on these tablets are sometimes schematic, sometimes quite life-like in appearance. It would be speculative to identify the former type with a particular class of weapon, or even to say that they stand for a distinct class; but the more representational ideograms show unmistakably the lateral bulges of the cruciform type in use at this time. A further question is whether these tablets do not record daggers rather than swords; there are plenty of cruciform daggers, as well as swords among the actual finds, most of the ideograms *look* more like daggers; and the group of signs regularly found beside them has been read by the decipherers as a form of the Greek word *phasgana*, which may originally have been used strictly for stabbing weapons or daggers.[20]

Side by side with the horned and cruciform swords in the warrior graves are found examples of the new type of large spearhead, a fearsome weapon.[21] It largely dispenses with the projecting socket of the Shaft-grave type, and yet it is no shorter; instead, the tube of the socket runs on in an unbroken line, with no perceptible neck, into the straight-edged blade, heavily midribbed to its tip. The midrib makes the blade more or less inflexible; the absence of neck means that it has no point of weakness where the head might snap off. In addition to their great weight in the thrust, these giant spearheads could probably be used in an emergency for a sideways cutting stroke. Their shafts were, sometimes at least, of olive-wood. They probably represent the main offensive weapon of the Palace period and may, indeed, ultimately explain the prestige that the spear holds in the Homeric poems as the heroic weapon *par excellence*. There is no higher praise for the Homeric hero than to be called 'famous with the spear', and the weapon is also stressed in general descriptions; for example, *Iliad* XIII, 340, where we are told that the battlefield 'bristled with the long, flesh-tearing spears that they grasped'. A broken Linear B tablet from Knossos records forty-two spears, but this was not the only form of spearhead used at this time. Smaller heads continue to appear in the graves, with normal, leaf-shaped blades; but the great 'one-piece' spearhead is the almost exclusive property of the Palace period.[22]

Archery in the Palace period, for whatever purpose, was certainly flourishing. The arrowheads themselves are as common as before, and still appear in flint and obsidian as well as bronze; but new evidence comes from a group of clay sealings found in the basement of a palace out-building at Knossos. These sealings carry an unmistakable arrow-ideogram, as does a broken tablet found near by which alone records 8,640 arrowheads, and had evidently been used to secure wooden chests full of the bronze 'arrow-plates'. Many of these were found *in situ*. As the building also contained tablets recording metals, chariots, wheels and spears, Evans named it the Armoury; whether or not this was accurate, the context does suggest that the arrowheads so carefully sealed, recorded and stored, were for public, and therefore presumably warlike, use. Also in the Armoury were tablets illustrated by a drawing of a pair of the horns of the Cretan wild goat. Since horn is the most important material used for composite bows, and since the Minoans certainly used a form of composite bow, Evans was probably right in associating these tablets also with Cretan archers.[23]

Our knowledge of the great advances made at this period in Mycenaean defensive armour dates, in the main, only from May 1960, when a remarkable discovery took place in a chamber tomb at Dendra, a few miles south-east of Mycenae.[24] A single warrior was buried here, and his bronze panoply lay separately, in the far corner of the tomb. Its main component was an elaborate bronze cuirass, consisting of a front and a rear plate, on to which were hung various supplementary pieces of armour: a high 'gorget' or neck-guard; two shoulder-guards ('pauldrons'), each with a smaller overlapping plate attached to protect part of the upper arm, and another triangular one in front where the pauldrons cross the chest; and at the bottom three curved overlapping plates ('taces'), back and front, to protect the lower part of the trunk. These are hung higher in front than they are behind, so as to facilitate movement of the legs. This is a striking piece of workmanship to find in any period of antiquity, but occurring as it does at the very beginning of the history of metal plate-armour, it almost surpasses belief. Perhaps its most surprising resemblance is to suits of armour dating from near the end of the age of plate-armour, such as that in the Musée d'Artillerie in Paris which was made for Louis XIV over 3000 years later.[25] Here we see similar breast- and back-plates, with pauldrons of almost identical shape attached; here again there are taces, also overlapping upwards since they have to contract from the hips to the waist. Yet over most of the intervening centuries, no such armour was in existence anywhere; this Mycenaean form of panoply was not copied by the Greeks, nor even perhaps by the later Mycenaeans, and the armourers of the Middle Ages and later can have had no inkling that the course along which their craft was being developed had been followed in the remote past. *Pl. 9*

The cuirass of Dendra was accompanied by other interesting finds, including two bronze objects which are almost certainly

1   Stele from Shaft-grave V at Mycenae. The carving in shallow relief shows a
warrior mounted in a light chariot drawn apparently by a single horse. He carries
a long tapered thrusting sword with a large pommel similar to several examples
recovered from the Shaft-graves. Neither he nor his opponent appears to be wearing
any armour. Sixteenth century BC. See p.20.

2   Blade of a bronze dagger inlaid with gold, silver and niello from Shaft-grave IV
at Mycenae. Hunters protected by shields of both the figure-of-eight and the straight-
sided variety are attacking lions with long spears. The archer must rely on his
companions' shields, as he carries none of his own. See pp. 17, 19-20.

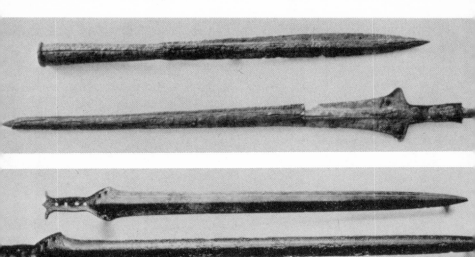

3-4 Mycenaean bronze 'one-piece' spear-head and swords. Spear-heads of this type, some 50 cm long, with socketed base and a strong mid-rib, belonged to a thrusting spear too heavy to throw. The upper-most sword is of the cruciform type, 61 cm long; the lower two are of the later form, today called the Griffzungenschwert, with a flatter cross-section: lengths 67 and 81 cm. See pp. 21-2; 28-9.

5-6 Ivory plaque from Delos showing an armed warrior. He wears a Minoan type of belt and a boars' tusk helmet, and carries a tall spear and a figure-of-eight shield (*left*). See pp. 19-20. *Below:* Clay tablet from Knossos inscribed with Linear B signs and ideograms, including those denoting a corslet, apparently of the Dendra type (see plate 9) and a chariot. See pp. 25, 27.

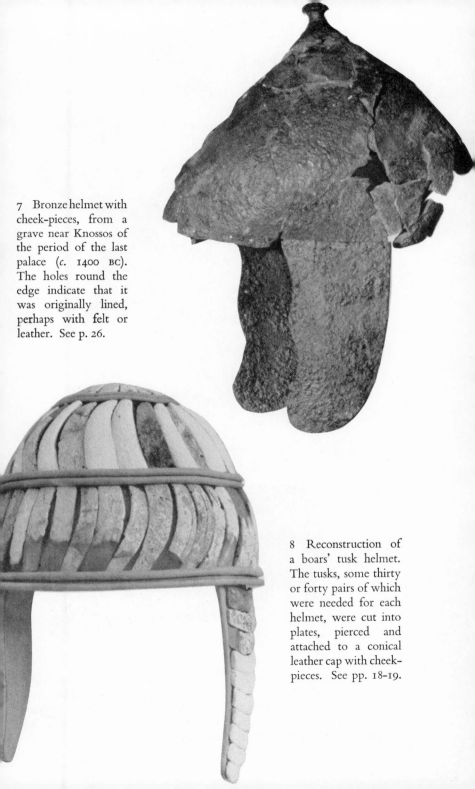

7 Bronze helmet with cheek-pieces, from a grave near Knossos of the period of the last palace (*c.* 1400 BC). The holes round the edge indicate that it was originally lined, perhaps with felt or leather. See p. 26.

8 Reconstruction of a boars' tusk helmet. The tusks, some thirty or forty pairs of which were needed for each helmet, were cut into plates, pierced and attached to a conical leather cap with cheek-pieces. See pp. 18-19.

9 Bronze plate-armour from a warrior's grave at Dendra. Of a considerably earlier date than the Warrior Vase, it shows an amazingly advanced technique on the part of the armourer, but this style of corslet was only in use for a limited time. Its weight may have rendered it impractical for use on foot in hot climates. Late fifteenth century BC. See p. 24.

the earliest examples of the metal greave, or shin-guard, known to us; but these were severely damaged. There is also strong circumstantial evidence that two damaged, but once splendid, swords were looted from this same tomb. The shape of the Dendra pauldrons shows that another object, found in 1939 in a somewhat earlier burial at Dendra and previously mis-interpreted as a helmet, was also a pauldron of slightly different form.[26] A similar cuirass must therefore have been buried here. This burial dates from about the middle of the fifteenth century BC; the Panoply tomb probably from the last quarter of that century.

Other traces of metal body-armour at this time come from a contemporary grave near the Minoan palace of Phaistos in Crete. A more recent discovery, so far only briefly reported, was made in the 'Arsenal' adjoining the Mycenaean palace at Thebes, where, together with many weapons, were found several of the subsidiary triangular plates, closely similar to those attached to the Dendra cuirass. The find belongs perhaps to the early fourteenth century, and confirms that the Palace period was prolonged until at least this date.[27]

The Knossos tablets extend the picture of this form of body-armour. In the west wing of the palace was found a large group of tablets showing chariots; the remainder of their contents is unfortunately a source of much controversy, but a number of them are inscribed with a further ideogram which Sir Arthur Evans, many years before either the discovery of an actual Mycenaean example or the decipherment of the script, identi-fied as a portrayal of a corslet. It appears only on these chariot-tablets, and a pair is regularly shown for each chariot; it was possibly worn only by chariot-borne troops. We do not know the word used for this type of cuirass at Knossos, but a sign-group which occurs on another, perhaps analogous, group of tablets has been read as e-po-mi-jo—'shoulder-pieces' or paul-drons.[28] Pl. 6

The Panoply tomb at Dendra also contained boars' tusks from a helmet, but with them were two cheek-pieces of bronze. If these were all from one helmet, this would suggest a process of translation into bronze carried part of the way only; if not, it shows at least that the old and the new materials were in use simultaneously. The hardest task, of beating a piece of bronze round to a conical or hemispherical shape to fit the skull, was achieved within the same period, not more than a generation or so later. A warrior grave at Knossos produced a helmet, still of almost identical shape with the boars' tusk type, but entirely of bronze, with separate bronze cheek-pieces.[29] The metal is thin, and the preserved parts of the helmet weighed only about 25 ounces, but there were perforations for the attachment of a lining. Pl. 7

On the other hand, helmets made entirely of boars' tusks were clearly still in use in the Palace period and later. But the type is no longer so predominant; representations, particularly in Crete, show 'built-up' helmets which share the horizontal bands of the boars' tusk type but are obviously of different material. The clearest portrayal, on a vase from Isopata near Knossos, suggests strips of leather supplemented by padding, and with ear-guards. Many helmets of this period have quite elaborate, tall crests. A helmet of perhaps deceptively advanced design, with a one-piece cap and hanging cheek-pieces, is worn by the boxers on a well-known stone relief vase from Hagia Triada near Phaistos; no such helmet is ever shown in a warlike context, and the material can hardly be metal.[30] Three Linear B tablets from Knossos record helmets of unknown material; the shape is evidently conical, with cheek-pieces, not unlike that of the bronze example from the same site, or of the boars' tusk variety.

Of the shield we see much less than in the Shaft-grave era; it is totally absent from the surviving tablets. One would assume that the great body-shield could be largely dispensed with, now that metal body-armour was available; but such representations as there are show that this form of shield was still known, in both 'figure-of-eight' and 'tower' form. In addition, the 'figure-of-eight' type had acquired both religious and purely decorative properties, which indeed it was to keep for centuries afterwards: a famous example is the colossal shield-fresco at the bottom of the Grand Staircase at Knossos.[31]

The chariot-tablets at Knossos have already been mentioned.[32] Altogether, the surviving tablets list over 400 chariots attached to the palace, and the presumed association with corslets in one group suggests that the context is military. The chariot-force was not kept in a state of complete readiness: the main fleet was evidently recorded, and perhaps kept, in the 'Armoury', and these either had their wheels removed for storage, the wheels being recorded separately, or were more fully dismantled; there is a different ideogram for each condition. The shape of the chariot is new, with a solid semicircular projection (not an open rail) at the back, probably on both sides. This is among the earlier appearances of the war-chariot in Crete, and it is possible that it was brought from the mainland by the Mycenaeans. Horses are also listed on some of the tablets with complete chariots and corslets. There is very little evidence indeed that the Mycenaeans or Minoans ever actually rode horses, in battle or elsewhere; they appear in art, as on the tablets, as traction animals, and the recent find of a number of bronze bits in the 'Arsenal' at Thebes, together with corslet-fragments and weapons, almost certainly testifies to this same use.

THE LATE PERIOD

The last considerable body of evidence belongs to the period in which the Mycenaean power, after reaching its greatest geographical extent, fell into a period of unrest and ultimately a series of disasters which engulfed most of the palaces and many other settlements on the Greek mainland. By this time Minoan Crete is no longer in the picture, either as a competitor or as a source of new developments. The Mycenaean horizon extends from Sicily and the Lipari Islands in the west, to Cyprus and Ras Shamra (on the Syrian coast) in the east; Mycenaean goods penetrate much farther, from Britain to Upper Egypt. To this period belongs the other main group of Linear B tablets, those found at the palace of Pylos in 1939 and later seasons of excavation. They were inscribed very shortly before the destruction, probably in about 1200 BC. Grave-goods continue to predominate among the other finds, but there is an important new source in the founders' hoards, a feature of this period in Greece.³³ These are collections of bronze tools, weapons and hardware generally, finished, unfinished or broken, which had evidently been collected by bronzesmiths as scrap-metal for re-working. A considerable proportion of our finds, no doubt including many of the hoards, dates from after rather than before the fall of the Mycenaean palaces; but the two outer limits of 1250 and 1150 BC will probably contain the bulk of the evidence.

A great change came over the Aegean world after the Palace period. In arms and armour this shows itself by the disappearance of the air of luxury which hung over the previous centuries. No longer do we find extravagantly adorned swords and daggers, huge shields, or panoplies in graves. The monarchs and the nobility are still in evidence, at least until the destruction of the palaces; but it seems that their traditional values have been pushed aside by the force of external circumstances, and by insecurity in particular. Nowhere is this better shown than in the development of swords. The great weapons of the sixteenth and fifteenth centuries have almost completely disappeared; swords are now shorter, stouter and more workmanlike, with strong hilting-devices and flattish, straight-edged blades. The most convincing reason suggested for this is that, with the decline in security as the eastern Mediterranean and Aegean were affected by new raids and migrations, it became common practice to carry a sword in everyday life, and for this purpose the splendid rapiers of earlier days had become too unwieldy and expensive. Some of the new swords are so short that they are difficult to distinguish from daggers and general-purpose knives or choppers, and the most characteristic sword of the late period did indeed develop from a short flat knife:³⁴ no example is as much as two feet long. A small specimen of this type even reached Pelynt in Cornwall. But this type of weapon was competing, ultimately without success, against a new and efficient sword that was standardized and mass-produced to a degree not before achieved in Greece; this is normally known by its German classification as the 'Griffzungenschwert'. It is distributed over an extraordinarily wide range of space and time, and it lives on, translated into iron, after the Bronze Age has ended.[35] It is found in many parts of Europe besides the Aegean; since the most numerous, best-made and probably earliest examples have occurred in Central Europe, it is now generally accepted that the sword developed there, perhaps in the Hungarian plain, although the bulk of the actual examples found in Greece were probably made locally. The fact that these swords appear in Greece distinctly before the fall of the Mycenaean palaces suggests that they were wielded by the Mycenaeans themselves, or possibly by European mercenaries in their service. The type had a flanged hilt—nothing new in itself—but with a distinctive, curvilinear outline and usually two 'ears' branching out at the top; the T-shaped cast pommel is abandoned. The weapon must have been superior to its rivals and not too difficult to produce, as is suggested by its simultaneous acceptance in Cyprus, the Levant and Egypt.

The latest Mycenaean spears in some ways repeat the story of the swords. Here again there is a sharp reduction in size and an elimination of ornament; the commonest type is medium-sized, with a leaf-shaped blade and a flat midrib extending to the tip. Again, there are at least a few examples which show associations with Central Europe, notably the spearheads with a flame-shaped outline to their blades. A handful of these have been found in Greece, mostly in the north-west; they were perhaps introduced by a route down the Adriatic.[36] Spearheads also provide evidence for strong links between Greece and Cyprus. Cyprus had long been of interest to the Mycenaeans as a source for the copper and tin which their bronze-based civilization so badly needed; but after about 1200 it is clear that large numbers of Mycenaeans were actually emigrating to Cyprus. Many objects of Mycenaean type appear in Cyprus now, and they include some small and rather crude reproductions of the great 'one-piece' spearheads of the Palace period (p. 23), long since out of date in Greece. Both Greece and Cyprus also adopt the bronze spear-butt, a spike with a hollow socket to fit on to the butt-end of the wooden shaft.[37]

For archery the evidence in the late period is unimpressive. The Mycenaeans had adopted (probably from Asia Minor) a true arrowhead with a large blade and thick tang, which fitted into a hole in the top of the shaft. One or two examples have been found which have a hollow socket instead of a tang. But the triangular arrow-plates or flat arrowheads (pp. 17, 23) remain vastly commoner, although now invariably of bronze. To the very rare portrayals of Mycenaean archers, we may add a fragment of a vase of the late thirteenth century from Iolkos in Thessaly, which shows part of the figure of a bowman in a line of marching warriors. Also used as a weapon in this period, and perhaps throughout Mycenaean times (if only rarely), was the sling.[38]

Defensive armour again shows a radical change, which in this case might seem to be a retrogression, in that metal plate-armour appears to go out of use. But there could be a variety of reasons for such a step, by no means all disadvantageous. To quote only one later parallel, the great 'Age of Plate' of the fifteenth and sixteenth centuries AD was brought to an end by a similar voluntary abjuration of plate-armour, for which the invention of gunpowder, though important, was far from being the only cause.[39] New developments in strategy, which entailed more forced marches, longer expeditions and generally greater mobility than before, would have been hindered by the weight of plate-armour, and were probably equally responsible for the change. From all that we know, it seems not unlikely that this consideration also applied in the thirteenth and twelfth centuries BC. If larger armies were also the rule now, this might well mean a lowering of the general standard of armour; the raw materials, and no doubt the skill, for bronze-working were always circumscribed in Mycenaean Greece.

The Dendra type of corslet is not seen, on surviving evidence, after the fourteenth century. Instead there are signs of a quite different form, or perhaps several forms, of body-protection. We see it in a famous painting on a bowl of the very latest Mycenaean period, the Warrior Vase found at Mycenae itself.[40] This vase shows the soldiers wearing stiff jerkins or corslets, which stand well out from the body but are almost certainly non-metallic, with decorated borders. These are worn with fringed skirts or kilts, which also have an outlined border and are in some cases dotted with white circles, probably representing the metal discs of a type of armour noted earlier (p. 18). The jerkins can be seen to possess long sleeves, of one piece with the body of the garment. Other fragments of vase-paintings confirm that this sleeved corslet was in common use, and the very indistinct ideogram on the Pylos tablets shows what appear to be short sleeves; the evidence for this type will then extend from rather before 1200 to decidedly later. The only likely relic of one of these corslets comes from a grave of the twelfth century at Kallithea in Achaea; here were found long thin strips of embossed bronze, suitable for attachment to a leather corslet, and perhaps represented by the outlined border of the Warrior Vase corslets.[41]

Most of the warriors in these scenes of the late period are wearing leggings, usually black with a band at the top. In one wall-painting the leggings extend from above the kneecap down to the ankle, and are painted white, but this need not indicate metal. A few pairs of bronze greaves survive from this period; they are merely elliptical plates of beaten bronze, bent over and laced up with wire, and less than a foot in height. Only one pair has been found in Greece itself, in the same grave at Kallithea as the corslet-fragments; the other two finds, which are a little earlier (about 1200), both occurred in graves at the site of Enkomi in Cyprus. (We have already noted signs of Mycenaean influence on Cypriot weapons at this time.) One example of a bronze ankle-guard has also been found in a Mycenaean tomb.[42] *Pls. 10, 11*

The Pylos corslet-tablets also illustrate what is evidently a helmet, placed above the corslet-ideogram to complete a set, but drawn in so schematic a way as to be impossible to identify. From vase-paintings, however, we learn of new helmet types at this period. Like the other armour, they are clearly in the main non-metallic; on both sides of the Warrior Vase they are shown running fore-and-aft in the manner of a deer-stalker, and dotted with white spots like the kilts worn by some of the same figures, which again is most likely to signify metal discs on a backing of hide or other animal-skin. Some of them also incorporate a prominent horn or tusk above the forehead piece; occasionally an unwrought boar's tusk has been found in Mycenaean graves, with or without the worked plates, and here we have a plausible illustration of its use. At the same time we must note that the traditional boars' tusk helmet could also occasionally survive: a second warrior grave at Kallithea, dating from well after the destruction of Pylos and most of the other great Mycenaean centres, produced cut plates on the old pattern.[43] This is a strikingly late context for a type which had been thought long obsolete, and it may help to explain the survival, in the Homeric *Iliad*, of a close description of one of these helmets (p. 19). The only sign of a metal helmet at this time is a bronze cheek-piece in the British Museum, the product of an unscientific excavation at Ialysos in Rhodes nearly a hundred years ago.[44]

For the shield of the late period, we at last have positive and consistent evidence. The great body-shield has now apparently gone, and in its place is shown a much smaller shield, held by a hand-grip. As in the previous period, the tablets give us no help, but the representations are clear. A small, circular shield is the commonest variety, but there are several uncanonical shapes.[45] The line of soldiers on the front of the Warrior Vase have roughly circular ones, but with a segment cut out of the lower edge; the men on the back have elliptical shields, and in one case a hand-grip is shown, unheld, which implies a neck-strap of the kind used with the body-shield. The warriors on the rather earlier fragments from Iolkos (*cf.* p. 30) have shields which again have recessed segments, but this time on each side; the effect is like a modified and drastically reduced form of the old figure-of-eight shield. These shields must all be largely of hide, like their predecessors, but they may have had a metal accessory in the shape of one or more large bronze discs, about six inches across, with a domed centre and sometimes a protruding spike. Such discs occur occasionally in warrior-graves from the latest Mycenaean period onwards; and although different explanations have been given for their use, it is now certain that some of them served as bosses for the outer face of a hide shield.[46] A twelfth-century grave at Mouliana in Crete produced the earliest specimens, but more impressive evidence comes from Cyprus in a slightly later period (see p. 44), a find which also shows that a metal border could be attached to such a shield.

The chariot is still very frequently seen; it is mentioned on the Pylos tablets, on palace wall-paintings at Mycenae and Tiryns, on a number of gems and painted potsherds, and on a whole class of Mycenaean vases of a degenerate style, found largely in Cyprus and Rhodes. The chariot design is in many ways old-fashioned when compared with those of contemporary chariot-using powers like New Kingdom Egypt and the Hittite Empire; it is now most often shown in processional use, but we may still imagine it as a military arm. Finally, it is of great interest that a vase from Crete, with the earliest (and very primitive) portrayal of an armed man on horseback, is now thought to date from the eleventh or tenth century. Here we are perhaps seeing Greek cavalry in its infancy.[47]

We can best sum up the developments in warfare in these years by returning once again to the Warrior Vase found in Mycenae and dating to its last days (p. 30). The figures on the vase are plain and unheroic; their armament is far from magnificence. But they are organized forces, in uniform equipment. The men on the reverse side have their spears raised, on the point of joining battle, but they are in step and move in unison. There could be no clearer portrayal of the change from the excessive individual splendour of the Shaft-grave princes to a standardized army. It is in some such array that we should imagine the Mycenaeans taking the field in the various wars of which we hear, in contemporary documents or in tradition, in the latter part of the thirteenth century.

Otherwise, we have seldom found an opportunity to consider Mycenaean arms in other than a fragmentary way, item by item; unfortunately, the evidence to justify talk of panoplies or tactics scarcely yet exists. For the Shaft-grave period we know little or nothing of the commoners; the only trustworthy picture transmitted to us is that of the princely champion duelling with his body-shield, boars' tusk helmet and rapier or long spear, but without metal armour, on foot or perhaps in a chariot. In the ensuing period, our broader-based evidence, and sudden advance in the understanding of it, add at least one new figure to the scene: the armour-plated and probably chariot-borne knight, no doubt of aristocratic but not generally of royal blood, superbly armed and so well protected that he could perhaps afford to dispense with a shield. Even the Linear B tablets do little to unify the disjointed picture and, at least until the closing years of the civilization, we are given no more than a glimpse of a Mycenaean battlefield as a whole. To attempt to fill in the blank spaces with the Homeric battle-scenes, which are true to no single phase of history, would be folly. As far as any historical sack of Troy is concerned, a glance at the Warrior Vase is not least valuable as an antidote to the poetic glories of the *Iliad*.

CHAPTER II

THE DARK AGE

THE FALL of the Mycenaean civilization, like that of the western Roman Empire some fifteen centuries later, was the prelude to a Dark Age. There are numerous similarities between the two periods, and a falling off in the use of armour would seem to be one of them. This, like many other inferences we might make about this period, is open to argument, for the lack of sound information about this first Dark Age is so acute that we can hardly obtain a true picture of it. It is possible that some of its darkness lies in the eye of the beholder, and that its poverty has been exaggerated by the poverty of our evidence. But the story that this tells, in Greece as in other parts of the eastern Mediterranean, is one of a sharp fall in material standards and, above all, in literacy. There are no traces of the art of writing in Greece from about 1200 to 750 BC, and when written texts reappear they are in an alphabetic script fundamentally different from Mycenaean Linear B. This does not, however, mean that there is necessarily no contemporary literary source at all, for the Homeric poems, although they were fashioned into their present shape only towards the end of the Dark Age, embrace earlier elements. Some of these, as we have seen, derive from the Mycenaean period; others may belong to the earlier part of the Dark Age, although this is almost impossible to prove in any particular instance.

Illumination of the Dark Age, therefore, still rests almost entirely with archaeology, but at this period its lantern is a dim one. For, together with the art of writing, most of the forms of representational art known to the Mycenaeans now appear to be lost. Frescoes, relief and inlaid metalwork, carved stones and figured scenes on vases all vanish for a time at least. Weapons and other artefacts are left to tell their somewhat arid tale. Yet from these we at once learn a striking fact: that the discovery of iron-working for utilitarian purposes, a supremely important innovation for the field of arms, took place in Greece near the beginning of the Dark Age. The Mycenaeans had known about iron, but largely as a material for decorative curios or amulets. Of their contemporaries farther east, the Hittites held a monopoly of the resources of iron ore then available; small quantities were exported to Egypt, Syria and elsewhere, and occasionally it was worked into serviceable objects—Tutankhamen, in the fourteenth century, had an iron-bladed dagger buried with him.[1]

It was from the Near East, too, that the knowledge of iron-working finally spread to Greece. Although a feature of the Dark Age in Greece was the almost complete suspension of foreign contacts, a steady trickle of trade seems to have been maintained with Cyprus, which was now, in part at least, a Greek-speaking island. There is first a transitional period, in the twelfth and early eleventh centuries, when the few iron implements found in Greece seem to be direct imports from at least the general direction of Cyprus. They include small iron knives with bronze rivets in the hilt, a sign of the tentative and restricted mastery of iron-forging techniques.[2] But before 1000 BC it becomes clear that the true Iron Age has arrived in Greece. There are still iron personal objects of a semi-decorative nature—for instance, long dress-pins—but the significant innovation is the appearance of fully-fledged iron weapons. The knowledge of iron-working, both in Greece and in the east, was applied to weapons relatively quickly, and before it was used for utilitarian tools—a sign, perhaps, that the age was an insecure one. Iron must soon have shown its superior properties as a material for weapons; although tougher and able to take a sharper edge if properly worked, it is in fact a lighter metal than the alloy bronze.

The first weapon to receive attention was the sword. It is clear that the bronze type known as the 'Griffzungenschwert' (p. 28) had proved the most efficient weapon of the Late Bronze

Age, and rare examples of it in bronze survive well into the Dark Age. When the transition to iron came, the shape of the 'Griffzungenschwert' was, not unnaturally, kept as far as possible. The very first Greek iron swords show certain peculiarities which link them with Cyprus and the Levant, where iron swords had appeared slightly earlier, and the earliest examples may have been imported from there. But soon Greek smiths no longer needed inspiration from outside: swords of the orthodox form reappear, and in the centuries that followed, it is astonishing to see how far this one shape dominates the swordsmith's production: in the 'Protogeometric' phase of the Dark Age, so called from that style of pottery which is current from the mid-eleventh century to about the end of the tenth, there is hardly a single sword known from Greece which is not of this form, and of iron. A few examples are very long and thin (one of them, at just under three feet, is longer than any bronze example of this type known from Greece), and were evidently too big to be fitted into the small cremation graves that were now common; accordingly they were bent into a circle or U-shape, an interesting example of the spoliation or 'killing' of weapons, a long-lived custom which often had a ritual purpose also. In the Geometric period, the ninth and eighth centuries, the sword becomes rather shorter and extremely stout; the pommel, no doubt of wood, was in the curving, half-moon shape that we see in the silhouette figures of warriors which begin to appear on Geometric pottery in the eighth century.[3] In Homer, swords and spearheads are without exception said to be of bronze when the metal is specified: one of the few cases of consistent archaizing in the poems. Observant critics have pointed out that some of the feats of arms in the *Iliad*—as when Achilles strikes a man on the neck (XX, 482) 'and sent his head, helmet and all, flying far away'—would be impossible with a bronze sword; but this tells us little, since it is anyway certain that Homer knew of the iron sword. It is more important to identify the background that he was trying to create, than to assess how far he succeeded.

Sometimes at least, the Greek warrior of the Dark Age carried a spear, as his Mycenaean predecessor had. But not until about

900 BC do we find a spearhead and sword in the same grave again; instead, the only recurrent combination is a spearhead and a short dagger.[4] The general scarcity of weapons in Early Iron Age graves is surely a sign of limited resources and, in particular, the spearhead-dagger combination suggests that the spear and sword, under the pressure of circumstances, may have become alternative weapons; separately, they are about as common as each other. It is possible to say that the transition from bronze to iron did not happen quite so early in spearheads as it did in swords; presumably the need was not so urgent. As a result, bronze spearheads of several late Mycenaean types were still being made in the Dark Age. But by the tenth century, the use of iron had come in for spearheads too; and for most of the Dark Age (though not thereafter) we find bronze heads only in outlying districts. The influence of Cyprus is again visible, before and after the change of metal; in Crete, where Cypriote links are often strongest, a group of long, thin pikes was found, imported from Cyprus where this weapon was perhaps known in antiquity as the *sigynna*.[5] But with these new varieties the old leaf-shaped spearhead continues to occur, translated into iron and elongated up to twenty inches or more. A recent grave-find in Macedonia gives us evidence for the size of the iron-tipped spear at this time: an iron head and butt were found *in situ* with traces of the wooden shaft running from one to the other, the grave being big enough to accommodate the spear unbroken. The head was about 11 inches long, the butt only $2\frac{1}{2}$, and the intervening shaft 6 ft. 2 in.—a total length of just over 7 ft. 3 in.[6]

From about 900 BC onwards, the practice of including two or three spearheads in a warrior-grave, often with no other arms, gradually became common in Greece.[7] By the late eighth century this custom was almost universal, and it continued sporadically thereafter. Sometimes there is one larger and one smaller spearhead, but more often, there are two or three of more or less identical size. Such multiple spears cannot be intended as a token of the deceased's wealth, as they were in the graves of Mycenaean kings and nobles. Almost certainly they mean something quite different: namely, that the tactics of long-range warfare had been adopted in Greece, with the spear being thrown as a javelin, so that two or more would be carried. There is some confirmation for this view at the end of the Dark Age, when battle-scenes appear on Geometric pottery, and we see figures transfixed by spears although no enemy is standing near them. The fact that men are still sometimes shown thrusting with a spear does not contradict this; no doubt a soldier would keep his last spear for hand-to-hand fighting. We should note that in the *Iliad*, too, the spear, a much emphasized weapon, is often thrown. Even Achilles, fighting with the huge ashen spear that only he could wield, repeatedly throws it; in his climactic duel with Hector (XXII, 273) he misses, and only recovers when Athena snatches it up and gives it back to him. Elsewhere, several heroes are armed with a 'pair of spears'. These seem to be features taken from warfare in the poet's own day.[8] *Pl. 13*

In such an era of missile fighting, we might expect to find the archer in his element, and the bow at least respected. As there is no representational evidence for most of the Dark Age (and, as always, no surviving bows), we must rely on the evidence of arrowheads, and the more interesting suggestions to be found in the Homeric poems.[9] The poet of the *Iliad* and *Odyssey*, although he quite frequently mentions the bow, both in general use and as the weapon of major figures like Paris, Teucer and Odysseus himself, represents it as of secondary importance in war. His descriptions, when they go into detail, point to the Asiatic composite type of bow which was foreign to Greece proper; but they also suggest incomplete understanding on the poet's part. The most detailed passage is the description of Pandarus' bow in *Iliad* IV, 105ff. It is made from the horns of a wild goat, sixteen hands across, 'which a horn-craftsman had worked over and fitted together, smoothing off the whole job and putting on a tip of gold'. Neither here, nor in the description of Odysseus' great bow (also made of horn) in *Odyssey* XXI, does Homer show awareness that a composite bow was not solid horn, but was made by letting strips of horn into a groove on the inner side of a wooden bow-stave, while dry sinew was moulded on to the outside. Still, his description may be elliptical, and does

not positively exclude this complicated process.[10] The evidence
of the arrowheads found is, in a negative way, very striking;
in contrast to the huge numbers of Mycenaean examples, those
from mainland Greece which date to the Dark Age can literally
be counted on the fingers of two hands. This may be partly because
arrowheads were no longer commonly included in graves,
which form our main source of information; and, in any case,
the picture does not apply to Crete, where arrowheads occur,
if less frequently than before, at intervals throughout the Dark
Age.[11] The commonest type here is the large tanged bronze
arrowhead, up to four inches in over-all length, which had come
to the Aegean in the Late Bronze Age (p. 29). In later days this
type, slightly modified, becomes closely associated with Crete
and appears on Cretan coins. The association probably goes back
to the Dark Age when, for a time at least, the science of archery
seems to have been kept alive in Crete.

By the eighth century, however, the bow had re-established
itself in mainland Greece. This is shown by a number of battle-
scenes on Attic Geometric vases, in which the bow appears,
nearly always with a distinctive double-curved form.[12] This
shape bears a fleeting resemblance to the well-known Scythian
'Cupid's Bow', an improved form of the composite bow which
was later to spread over much of western Asia and eastern Europe.
But this is an improbably early date for the Scythian type to have
reached Greece, and it seems easier to believe that the Geometric
artists are really portraying a much simpler type, an all-wooden
or 'self' bow with an inward curve half-way down the stave.
The Cretans had used this type since Minoan times, but they
had also mastered the production and use of a kind of composite
bow, potentially more powerful but requiring specialist skill
in the archer, as well as the bowyer who made it. We may imagine
exponents of more primitive weapons, such as stone-throwers,
not necessarily with the specialist skill needed for the use of the
sling, fighting alongside the archers of the Dark Age. Axes, too
have occasionally turned up in warrior graves, and it is possible
that these were taken into battle; they appear, after all, in the
Iliad (XIII, 612; XV, 711). *Pl. 35*

10-11 Front and side views of a late Mycenaean krater, the Warrior Vase. It indicates that uniform equipment was now in use, with lighter, mainly non-metallic helmets, armour and shields. See pp. 30-33.

12 Fragment of a Geometric krater of about 750 BC showing a two-horse chariot or wagon, possibly used only to transport the warrior to the field of battle. The warriors here carry the curious 'Dipylon' type of shield. See pp. 44-6.

13-14 Three iron spear-heads of socketed type, about 40 cm long, from a Late Geometric tomb at Argos (*left*). See pp. 38-9. *Below:* Fragments of the bronze mountings and bosses from a shield found at Kaloriziki in Cyprus. Eleventh century BC. See p. 44.

15-16 Bronze votive figurine of a warrior found at Delphi (*above*). He wears a Corinthian helmet, one of the earliest known representations of the type. Early seventh century BC. See p. 51. *Right:* Seventh century bronze figure of a warrior in the heroic tradition from Karditsa; he wears a metal belt and carries a 'Dipylon' shield on a strap over his shoulder. See pp. 42, 44-5.

17 Bronze panoply from a Late Geometric warrior's grave in Argos. The helmet is of a primitive shape with a high crest, but the bell-shaped corslet is of a style which was to remain unchanged for many years. See pp. 41, 43, 50.

18-19 *Below, left:* Inside of a hoplite shield, showing the bronze fitting (*porpax*) through which the left forearm passed, enabling the left hand to grasp a handle (*antilabē*) on the inside of the shield-rim. *Below, right:* Front view of a similar shield, captured at Pylos in 425 BC. See pp. 53, 105.

For armour in the Dark Age, the picture remains an almost total blank. This might mean only that there was no *metal* armour, not that there was none at all. Since the recent discoveries of Mycenaean armour, which in some cases bears resemblances to that of the later Greeks, more scholars have become inclined to believe that there was some continuity from one to the other, running right through the Dark Age; just as in architectural features, in artistic conventions and motifs, and above all in saga, mythology and religion, there seem to be clear and direct links between Mycenae and later Greece, even though there is a large break in the evidence. The attractively simple explanation, that art did survive throughout but only in perishable materials, or that the buildings of the intervening period happen not to have been found by us, may well hold good in these instances; but it can hardly be valid in the case of bronze armour.

The facts are that the bronze plate-corslet, the most substantial piece of armour, does reappear in Greece near the end of the eighth century, when it is found in a grave at Argos;[13] and that it does reproduce, in developed form, the basic features of the inner cuirass of the Dendra armour of 700 years earlier. Most of the intervening period in Greece seems to be devoid of such plate-armour; yet in geographical terms Dendra and Argos are a bare ten miles apart. Can there be a link? It seems to me impossible that there was direct descent and, if we were right in thinking that even the later Mycenaeans preferred a non-metal corslet (p. 30), this view will be much reinforced. But to the north of Greece the situation was very different. In time, the Dark Age of Greece falls in the middle of a long and apparently prosperous culture-phase, centred in the middle and upper Danube: the Urnfield period, a feature of which is the varied bronze industry. The Urnfield peoples and their predecessors had been in prolonged contact with the Mycenaeans, and there was a substantial two-way trade in artefacts between Greece and Central Europe. It is very likely that the bronze plate-corslet was one of the commodities included in this traffic, for a whole series of bronze cuirasses has been found on sites in Central Europe, France and Italy.[14] If most of these date from very late in the Urnfield period, an example found a few years ago at Čaka in Czechoslovakia is much earlier, and must belong in the vicinity of 1200 BC. But all these finds, like the Argos one, were of cuirasses alone; none was associated with the subsidiary plates of the Dendra type of armour. This fact, and the historical situation in eighth century Greece, make it quite credible that the Argos corslet (with, no doubt, its lost contemporaries in Greece) was freshly modelled on the European type, which the Greeks must have encountered at this time in their colonial ventures in Italy. (Specimens of the European corslet have been found at Naples and in Etruria.) As with the art of writing in Greece before and after the Dark Age, so with armour there is a change in attitude as well as a *lacuna* in time; and these together argue strongly against continuity.

On the question of other, non-metal armour, one can only guess. Not only is it untraceable in the actual remains, but the representations on vases when they reappear are in a silhouette style which cannot indicate the presence of body-armour. It is true that there are statuettes from the eighth century on which show warriors naked apart from a thick belt round the waist, apparently of bronze;[15] and possibly such belts were worn for protection in battle, over normal clothing or leather jerkins. The bronze greave, which does eventually return to Greece, is only detectable after the end of the Dark Age; here, too, there is a slight change in form from the Mycenaean type. *Pl. 16*

Helmets tell a somewhat different story. For one thing, there are the remains of a solitary metal helmet, found in a grave at Tiryns, which date from the phase after the final break-up of Mycenaean culture, about 1100 BC or even later.[16] It is unlike any of the Mycenaean types known to us, but the cheek-piece, with its crenellated front edge, recalls that of the bronze helmet from Knossos. This is the last sign of the survival of the armourer's skill for several centuries, but the metal helmet, just as it had apparently been the last piece of armour to go from Greece, does seem to be the first to return. There are possible indications of its presence on figurines, usually of bronze, which certainly begin not much later than 800.[17] Many of these wear prominent helmets, sometimes crested; and while one cannot be certain of the intended material of the helmets, the plain conical shape, which is commonest, is very like that of the contemporary metal helmet in Syria and other parts of the Near East. The parallel can be pressed more closely, because the two commonest forms of crest which surmount these helmets, one curving forwards over the head, the other running fore-and-aft supported by a stilt, are also present in Near Eastern representations, particularly those of Assyrian soldiers on stone reliefs. Another primitive form of helmet is sometimes seen on the statuettes, shaped like an inverted hemispherical bowl, and again with a crest, or at least a peak, on the crown. But the conical shape is commoner, and is also seen on the roughly contemporary pictures of warriors on Geometric vases. The helmet is first invisible in the silhouette, and can only be detected by its plume, but presently a high crest appears and a hint of the sharper outline of the helmet is suggested. Finally, in the same grave at Argos which produced the corslet (p. 41), there is at last an actual example of a bronze helmet.[18] It is a variety of the conical type, and its splendid arching crest-holder is still preserved, very close in shape to one seen on an Assyrian relief of a generation earlier. Basically it is a high cap, with a forehead-guard, two cheek-pieces and a neck-guard riveted on at the appropriate places round the lower rim. The helmet must have been imposing but quite impractical, being top-heavy and not very protective. In the *Iliad*, bronze helmets are common among the leading figures, and they sometimes have a tall crest which 'nods menacingly from above'; the most familiar example is Hector's, which alarms his baby son Astyanax in *Iliad* VI, 469ff. It is hard for us to say whether such details are inspired by the long-lost equipment of Mycenae, or by the new types which were perhaps beginning to appear in the poet's own day. *Pl. 17*

The helmet from Argos is merely the first known example of a group which takes us out of the Dark Age and into the ensuing period. We have still to consider the shield of the Dark Age, and here at last we find a continuous strand which runs through from late Mycenaean times to the eighth century. In representations, the small round shield of the latest figured vase-paintings of Mycenae (p. 32) is very much like a form of shield shown by the Geometric artists. Both probably had a single central grip, enabling the shield to be held at arm's length when necessary— as when Deiphobus, in the battle at the ships, 'held his leather shield away from him, in fear of the doughty Meriones' spear' (*Iliad* XIII, 163). But a more substantial link is provided by the bronze bosses. Admittedly, these could at times be used for purposes other than warfare, but their connection with shields is proved by a grave-find in Cyprus at the site of Kaloriziki near Kurion.[19] Many years ago this tomb was looted and a splendid gold sceptre taken from it; but in 1953 it was rediscovered and several objects, missed by the looters and lying in their original position, were found. Among them were three of these bosses, one large between two smaller ones, with fragments of a bronze rim of curious shape running round them. The whole thing has been convincingly restored as a broad shield with a W-shaped lower outline, rather like those on the front of the Warrior Vase (p. 32). This princely tomb, probably of a Mycenaean immigrant, is to be dated between 1100 and 1050 BC. From then onwards, at intervals through the Dark Age, similar bosses occur both in Greece and in Cyprus. Often they are in warrior graves of modest type, but they are now almost always found singly, suggesting a smaller, probably round shield, the basic material of which must be hide. *Pl. 14*

This was not the only type of shield known to Greece, at least by the end of the Dark Age when Geometric figure-painting begins. The artists show a round and a rectangular shield, of moderate size, carried by warriors who have both arms free— a sign that the neck-strap or *telamon* was still in use, no doubt supplemented by a handle. But most frequent and most baffling of all is the great 'Dipylon' shield, so called because it is regularly carried by the warriors on a group of vases of about 750-725, found in the Dipylon cemetery at Athens.[20] This is something less than a body-shield, since it never reaches the knees, but it is often shown enormously wide at the top and bottom, with the sides curving sharply inwards to a narrow waist at the middle.

Even allowing that its shape has been exaggerated by the artists, can one believe in this extraordinary shield? It might be explained as originally a stretched animal-hide with the four legs projecting. But in the seventh century and later, a less exaggerated form of this shield became the standard 'property' for artists who wished to depict a heroic scene, such as Ajax or Achilles fighting at Troy. It was evidently accepted as a suitable accessory for a hero when it was no longer used in real life. As a motif, it lived on for centuries—for instance, as a device on Boeotian coins. Even in the eighth century, it may already have acquired romantic associations and been used by the Geometric artists in a similar way. In this case, it may well represent a distorted reminiscence of the 'figure-of-eight' body-shield of the Minoans and Mycenaeans. One link between them is that both also acquired sacred properties; and from what we know, it was in character for the Geometric artists to dwell on past glories. All these shield-forms, however, real or otherwise, were about to be displaced by the new, large round shield of the hoplite, which was to dominate Greek warfare in the ensuing centuries. *Pl. 16*

It remains to say something of the horse and chariot in the Dark Age. We found almost no evidence for Mycenaean equitation of any kind, and there is no question of their having ridden chargers into battle; the chariot, on the other hand, even if it was used solely for its prestige value, had been taken seriously as a war arm. In the Dark Age, the situation is almost reversed, for while there is no good tradition that war-chariots were used at this time, we learn from several authors (Aristotle is the most respected of them) that cavalry dominated warfare in Greece in the period before the rise of the hoplite, which began in about 700 BC. This is surprising, but there is some confirmatory evidence for it. In the Geometric vase-paintings, we see helmeted warriors holding horses' heads; even if these might still be explained as chariot-horses, there are a few late scenes which show armed men actually riding.[21] Certainly cavalry became most strongly established in the fringes of the Greek world—in the cities of the Asia Minor coast, where Greeks were now permanently settled and in contact with Anatolian peoples who rode, and in

Thessaly. Farther east, in Cyprus, Greeks even now fought in chariots; but otherwise the position of the chariot in Greek warfare is ambiguous after the Bronze Age.[22] It is a favourite subject of the Geometric artists, but like their Mycenaean ancestors they almost always show it in processions or, as some have thought, in races. Sometimes it has a long body, like that of the vehicle used for carrying the bier at funerals, and at times it seems to have four wheels, which makes it less a war-chariot than a wagon. If it was used in war at all, it can only have been as a wagon for transporting the richer warriors. Its rare appearances in battle-scenes can be explained as another example of heroic or romanticized art; indeed one such scene, showing a pair of Siamese twins making a fighting retreat to a chariot, has been convincingly identified with an episode narrated by Nestor in the eleventh book of the *Iliad*, and set in a period well before the Trojan War:

'Fifty chariots I took ... and I should have killed the twins, Aktorione-Molione, had not their father, the Earthshaker, saved them out of the battle' (XI, 747).

Elsewhere in his reminiscences, Nestor is beaten in a chariot-race by the twins 'because of their number' (XXIII, 638). *Pl. 12*

Any attempt to give a unified account of warfare in the Dark Age must reckon with difficulties far greater than even those present in Mycenaean times. For the eleventh, tenth and ninth centuries, with neither writers nor artists to portray contemporary fighting, we are hard put to it to give even the most generalized summary, beyond saying that, unless the graves are grossly misleading, warfare was as sharply affected by the impoverishments of the time as any other activity. In a cremation of about 900 BC under the later market-place at Athens (Tomb XXVII), were found a long sword, a larger and a smaller spear, sundry tools and a pair of horse-bits, all of iron. In the twin spears we may see the use of a javelin, in the twin bits perhaps a symbol of twin horses and thus of a funerary cart or chariot. But does the absence of shield or armour mean what it suggests? Would *any* further inference be justified? And this is one of the very richest graves of these centuries; the most that we find elsewhere is the combination of spear and shield-boss.

Only about the middle of the eighth century, with the appearance of battle-scenes on vases and the virtual certainty that some details of Homer's descriptions are taken from this, his own lifetime, does light return. The pattern of warfare can now be seen to have changed fundamentally since our last clear sight of it in the late Mycenaean times. There is no sign of uniformity or organization now. The battles are indiscriminate affairs, partly of missile-warfare with archery prominent, partly of sword- and spear-fights. The scene is often set at the beaching of a warship, a new motif. We do not know, and may never know, how far backwards in time we may extend this eighth-century picture, nor how far forwards that of the late Mycenaean period. The lack of earlier evidence for missile-warfare in the one case, the lack of later armour in the other, are equally strong deterrents to further surmise.

CHAPTER III

THE AGE OF THE HOPLITE

TECHNICALLY, the Dark Age may be said to have ended when alphabetic inscriptions begin to appear in Greece. This event roughly coincides with the major revival of representational art in the region of 750–725 BC, and with a more general upheaval which must have affected most aspects of Greek life. One can also see, in these years, the first glimmerings of a revolution in armour and weapons which was to affect Greece permanently; and it is fortunate that these signs are present, because at about 700 a change in Greek customs took place which, although perhaps insignificant historically, is from our point of view serious. This was the widespread abandonment of the practice of burying men with their arms. This means, not that the total surviving quantity of weapons and armour falls away—far from it—but that the uniquely valuable evidence of a grave-group, which as a rule can be dated accurately and gives a homogeneous picture of the equipment of a single warrior, is henceforward lost to us. The actual specimens of arms and armour now come in the main from a new source, the great sanctuary-sites, at which the Greeks would dedicate objects of daily use, and especially arms. In early times these were normally spoils, won from enemies, and perhaps previously erected to form a trophy on the battlefield; but by the Hellenistic period at least the habit of dedicating one's own armour, in gratitude for its protection, had arisen. The most important of these sanctuaries, Olympia and Delphi, were centres of Panhellenic and indeed international standing, and the offerings there were drawn from a correspondingly wide area. Other sites, like the sanctuaries of Athena at Lindos, Hera on Samos, Artemis at Sparta or Apollo at Bassae, have yielded finds of more obviously local character. But these finds are seldom closely datable. The common sequence of events at a sanctuary was that, over the years, dedications were hung or heaped up until the place became intolerably cluttered, when they would be thrown out. Occasionally they were put to some use, however humble, as at Olympia, where pieces of armour were often used as filling-material for the banks of earth round the stadium on which the spectators sat. More often they were simply dumped into disused wells, rivers or specially dug pits. As a result, finds of widely different date are often found piled up together. But this loss is more than compensated for by the continuous advances made by Greek artists of the Archaic and Classical periods. The swift mastery of outline painting and incision on vases, of repoussé metal-work, of clay modelling and, later, of stone sculpture and hollow-cast bronzes—all this gives a uniquely rich array of representational evidence for armour, as for many other aspects of contemporary Greek life.

THE COMING OF THE HOPLITE

The rise of the fully-armed Greek infantryman, the *hoplitēs*, is the thread which runs through and unifies this period of the development of arms.[1] While the various elements of the complete bronze panoply were being invented, borrowed or revived in Greece, the economic resources of cities and individuals were growing, until it was found possible for the richer states to raise whole armies of men equipped, normally at their own expense, with plate-armour. A simple but effective tactical formation, the close-packed phalanx, was developed and universally accepted as the proper way to deploy such troops. These changes once made, Greek warfare slipped into an extraordinarily rigid framework, which lasted for more than 300 years. The hoplite was, of course, not the only type of soldier used in this period, but in status and effectiveness he was supreme. In all Greek art there are few subjects so popular as the hoplite, whether arming, departing to war, fighting or dying. Historically, the sufficiency of the hoplite was such that, after dominating Greek battlefields for two centuries (and foreign ones too, when Greeks or other hoplites could be induced to serve as mercenaries), he could still play the major part in defeating the Persian land forces, against heavy numerical odds, at the battles of Marathon and Plataea.

It is certainly surprising to find that the hoplite developed so early, but we should not imagine that he was created in a day. Even at this period of sudden and interacting changes, it is unthinkable that all the technological, tactical and social developments, which were necessary before a hoplite phalanx could be put in the field, happened in one sweep of a hand. Our safest guide lies in the elements of the panoply, as they severally make their appearance on the Greek scene, in actual finds or in art. The warrior grave at Argos (p. 41), alone in the Geometric period, produced recognizable bronze armour: a roughly bell-shaped bronze corslet composed of a breastplate and backplate, with slotted attachments down the side, and a tall crested helmet. The corslet is one of the most striking discoveries from its period, partly because it is such a competent piece of work; yet no immediate ancestor can be found for it in Greece. This phenomenon is explained, if we are right to connect it with the earlier bronze corslets from other parts of Europe. Certainly if it came from outside Greece, it came from there; for the great civilizations of the East which now, as often before, were contributing so much to Greek culture, apparently never adopted bronze plate-armour. Probably the hot climate is an adequate explanation of this; at all events the Egyptians, Assyrians and other Oriental peoples seem to have been content with scale-armour, or simply linen or leather. But in Greece the plate-corslet was found so satisfactory that it was worn by hoplites for two centuries, with only the slightest modifications of the type found at Argos, and then discarded shortly before the Persian Wars. The Argos corslet is thus a notable landmark for Greece.

The helmet found with it has a different history. As an artefact it is much less impressive (p. 43), being of faulty design and constructed out of quite simple parts, riveted together. Not surprisingly, it had a short life; only a handful of examples are known, mostly from Olympia,[2] and there are already signs of the presence of a vastly superior form of helmet in Greece. This is first seen on a vase of about 700 BC, and on bronze figurines not far from the same date.[3] The helmet is a remarkable one: in a single sheet of metal it covers almost the whole head from the collar-bone upwards. The cheek-pieces, instead of hanging, merely sweep forwards continuing the lower rim of the helmet, and leave only a small, roughly T-shaped aperture for the eyes, nose and mouth. All round the rim are a series of perforations for the attachment of an inner lining. Some of the actual helmets found are very close in detail to those on the figurines; one or two must, on grounds of style, be even earlier.[4] There are good reasons for thinking that this was the helmet that the ancient Greeks called the Corinthian. Herodotus (IV, 180) mentions the name once, and we see it first and most frequently on Corinthian pottery; thereafter it becomes the most conspicuous possession of the Greek hoplite. From the beginning, it can have two kinds of crest, one lying directly along the crown, the other of a form already seen, high and curling forward at the top. *Pl. 15*

Technologically, the helmet is such an advanced product that it deserves a closer look. To beat a complete head-piece out of one sheet of bronze has always been a feat requiring exceptional skill on the part of a smith; in the seventeenth century AD, for instance, armourers seem to have lost this art, and resorted to constructing helmets in two or more pieces with a join over the crown; while even in 1939 a modern Greek artificer, making a replica of a similar form, found it difficult to beat out the back of the helmet unless a deep recess was left over the forehead.[5] So far as we can tell, the Greek bronzesmiths at the end of the eighth century had no foreign model or precedent for their achievement. There is even one contemporary monument which records this step: a crude bronze figurine of a bronzesmith beating out a Corinthian helmet on a high 'rod'-anvil. So effective an invention was this helmet that more than 2000 years later its design was quite closely copied in a type of helm worn in fifteenth-century Italy.[6] *Pl. 20*

The Corinthian helmet, though widely accepted, never entirely excluded other forms in Greece. One reason may have been that, for all its protectiveness, it must have made its wearer temporarily deaf, besides sharply restricting his vision. Another force behind the appearance of different types was the growth of regionalism, a phenomenon which had largely developed in the Dark Age of Greece. But the regional names given to other forms of Greek helmet, in most cases, rest on no ancient authority as 'Corinthian' does; they are merely guesses based on the distribution of examples or representations, and some of them are demonstrably wrong. The earliest case of regional peculiarity is a very simple kind of helmet which the Cretans developed from the Geometric type in the shape of an inverted bowl (p. 43); the back of the helmet is gradually brought down, to give greater protection and stability and there is always a high crest. At several Cretan sites, tiny miniatures of this type were dedicated. As it is also found in the art of other Aegean islands, and only very rarely on the main-land, 'Insular' is as good a name as any for this type. It was a primitive form, and did not even last through the seventh century; no life-sized examples have been found.[6] Pl. 33

Another common form, superficially similar to the 'Insular', is the so-called 'Illyrian' helmet, in fact a purely Greek type which perhaps originated somewhere in the Peloponnese in the earlier seventh century, and only centuries later found its way to Illyria and other barbarian lands. It too leaves the wearer's face open, but it has a distinct cheek-piece projecting downwards from the head-piece, as well as the low neck-guard. The helmet was made in two pieces, joining over the crown. The crest was always of the kind which lay directly on the helmet; thus it protected the one point of weakness, and the parallel ridges which kept the crest in place are a good identifying feature.[7] Pl. 23

This, then, was the range of helmet-types available to the Greek hoplite in the early years; later, as we shall see, new varieties were added and the old ones modified. The remaining piece of armour regularly worn on the body was the greave, but it seems to have been a little later in making its appearance. We first see it on vases of about 675 BC, picked out by incision or painted a distinctive white. Here again, there are definite differ-ences from the known Mycenaean greaves, which make con-

20-21 *Right:* The 'Corinthian' was the commonest form of helmet in the age of the hoplite. It was beaten out from a single sheet of bronze and represents a considerable advance in technique. See pp. 51, 93. *Below:* The backplate of a bronze 'bell' corslet from a dedication at Olympia. Late seventh century. See p. 50.

22 Shield-blazon in the form of a winged horse, from Olympia. These shield devices may have helped to identify the bearer when his face was largely hidden by his helmet, and many different motifs are found among the votive deposits and shown in art. See pp. 54–5.

23 Bronze helmet of the so-called 'Illyrian' type. This helmet was made in two pieces, the weak area of the join being strengthened by the crest. Late sixth century. See p. 52.

24 Bronze helmet of the 'Chalcidian' type. Closely related to the Corinthian form, this helmet had the advantage of leaving the wearer's ears unobstructed. Sixth century BC. See pp. 69-70.

25 Small pottery flask (*aryballos*) in the shape of a head wearing an Ionian helmet. The cheekpieces of these helmets were separately made and sometimes hinged to the main part. About 600 BC. See p. 65.

26, 28 *Above:* Projected scene of a mixed, perhaps heroic, battle, on a Protocorinthian aryballos from Lechaion. See p. 57. *Below, right:* Corinthian alabastron painted with typical hoplite equipment of the late seventh century, including throwing and thrusting spears, helmet, corslet and greave. See pp. 50-5.

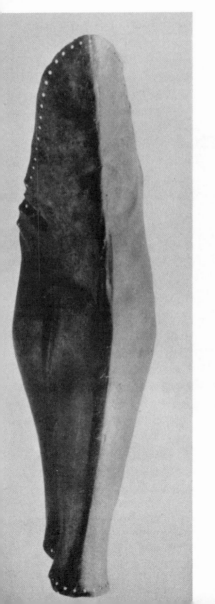

27 Bronze greave from Olympia. Carefully moulded to fit the muscles of the wearer's leg, it originally had a fabric lining attached by means of the perforations visible at the upper and lower edges. See p. 53.

29-30 *Above:* Late seventh-century plate from Rhodes showing the epic theme of Hector and Menelaus fighting over the fallen Euphorbus. *Below:* Upper frieze from a Protocorinthian olpe, the 'Chigi' vase. A boy flute-player provides martial music for a phalanx of hoplites moving into battle in close formation. See pp. 58, 68.

31 Fragment of an Etruscan funerary cippus now in the museum at Palermo. The relief decoration on these small stone blocks often gives a representation of the deceased; this example probably belonged to a soldier, as it shows mounted warriors armed in the Greek style. The Etruscans adopted this type of armour as a result of their contacts with their southern neighbours in the Greek colonies of Magna Graecia. See p. 75.

32 Decorated helmet from Axos in Crete. In the seventh century the islanders, always intensely individualistic, produced their own variation on the Corinthian style of helmet, without a nose-guard or a curved lower rim. This helmet, like other armour made in Crete at the time, was ornamented with beautifully executed repoussé relief which, in this case, repeats the winged horse motif seen on the shield blazon from Olympia. See pp. 63-4.

33　The Trojan Horse, from a seventh-century relief-decorated pithos from Mykonos. The artist has made no attempt to depict the weapons of the heroic age; these warriors have Corinthian and 'Insular' helmets, and carry a round shield with one or two spears, or a sword. See pp. 52, 57.

tinuity unlikely. The greave is now longer, running from the top of the kneecap to the instep, and there is no sign of decoration or of wire laces. Probably rather later in the seventh century, actual specimens begin to occur to supplement the evidence of the vase-paintings; these develop into beautiful pieces of workmanship, shaped to the anatomy of the human leg and beaten to a thinness which allowed them to be simply 'snapped' on, as later representations show.[8] *Pl. 27.*

But the most important single item in the panoply of the hoplite, from which indeed he took his name, was the great round shield or *hoplon*.[9] It was much larger than the round shield of the preceding era: the regular diameter is about three feet, and one exceptional example was found to be nearly four feet across. The shape is gently convex, except that the rim is usually flat. The basic material was wood, reinforced with bronze. The whole shield sometimes had a bronze facing, and the rim was invariably faced with bronze, usually with a repoussé cable-decoration. On the inner side was a bronze strip, sometimes short but more often running right across the shield, and bowed out in the middle to form a loop through which the left forearm was passed, up to just below the elbow. This arm-band, or *porpax* as the Greeks called it, was a new invention and peculiar to this kind of shield. At the edge of the shield—the right-hand edge as seen from inside—was a handle, the *antilabē*, a leather thong which was gripped by the left hand. This two-handled arrangement had many advantages: it helped to relieve the great weight of the shield, it enabled the soldier to release the *antilabē*, if he wanted to hold a spare weapon, without losing his shield, and it made it possible to hold the shield rigidly in an oblique position so that the enemy's weapons would glance off it. The *telamon*, or sling, for the heavy shield had finally been abandoned, which meant that the shield could no longer be left to hang from the back; this mattered especially on those regrettable occasions when the hoplite had to flee, and it was the standard practice then to throw the shield away—or so one would gather from the repeated appearance of this theme in the poets, beginning with Archilochus:[10] *Pls. 18, 19*

'Some Saian is rejoicing in my shield, which I unwillingly left by a bush—a piece of armour in perfect condition! But I saved myself. Perish that shield, I'll get another just as good.'

Such nonchalance would have been impossible in Sparta, where keeping one's shield was synonymous with keeping one's honour, as we are reminded by the story of the Spartan mother who enjoined her son to come home either with his shield or on it.

The hoplite shield had, in common with some other types, the weakness that it gave one-sided protection; in a frontal attack, the hoplite could put his left shoulder forward and draw his unprotected right side back, or, as was more usual in the phalanx, keep so close to his neighbour on the right as to be covered by the overlapping left-hand part of his shield (cf. p. 105). But occasionally he might be forced to carry out a manoeuvre which involved turning his unshielded side towards an enemy—most obviously, when moving to the left in column from in front of the enemy. The danger of such a move when faced by a quick-thinking commander of mobile troops was shown in a memorable way by the rout of the Athenian hoplites before Amphipolis in 422 (Thucydides V, 10: cf. p. 105).

This apart, the hoplite shield was a most successful device. Although large round shields had been used earlier by the Assyrians and some of their neighbours, the handles were the key factor and they seem to have been an original Greek invention. Of all the military innovations of this era, it was the hoplite shield which lasted longest. It is frequently mentioned in ancient sources as the 'Argive' shield; it may be that this name is an accurate reminiscence, and that the design was originally produced at Argos. Some confirmation has been found in the decoration of the metal strip running across the inside, the style of which could well be Argive. The other invariable feature of this shield was the blazon or device on the front. Where the shield was faced with bronze, this was probably painted on; otherwise a cut-out silhouette in bronze, often with engraved detail, could be attached to the wooden facing; a number of such blazons have been found at Olympia.[11] The original object of these was, perhaps, like that of the heraldic devices of medieval knights, to identify the wearer, whose features would often be hidden by the Corinthian helmet. On early vases, each hoplite seems to have his individual badge, most commonly in the form of an animal or bird. Later, with the development of democracy, it was the more frequent practice for hoplites to carry the uniform device of their city (p. 67). Already on vases of the Late Geometric period, from about 725, men are shown carrying blazoned round shields; these are very likely to be of the hoplite type, but certainty is possible only when, a generation or more later, we are shown the inside view with the distinguishing arm-band and hand-grip. A warning should be given about one very common feature of battle-scenes on vases and elsewhere, from the early seventh century onwards: the entirely mythical shield which is a variant of the 'Dipylon' form mentioned earlier (pp. 44–5), but turned on its side. It is now usually called the 'Boeotian' shield since it is a common device on the coins of that region.[12] It retains the two arcs, cut inwards from the circumference, but in a much reduced form; in over-all shape it is often almost circular, and it further apes the hoplite shield by acquiring a blazon on the outside, and a *porpax* and *antilabē* inside, whereby it is held in its incongruous sideways position. It remains a favourite device of Greek artists for centuries, and is usually a sign that the scene is taken from heroic saga. In actual fact it can never have existed, even if its immediate predecessor did. *Pl. 22*

This was the extent of the regular armour of the hoplite, and the other garments that he wore were mostly taken from everyday life. Some seventh-century vases show hoplites wearing what looks like a kind of leather codpiece below the corslet, but before 600 this gives way to a short tunic, worn underneath the corslet but only visible where it hangs below the waist like a kilt. We should not believe those vase-painters who, throughout the Classical period, show warriors fighting bare below the belt or even stark naked. The broad metal belt of the previous period (p. 42) may have afforded some protection to the stomach in battle, but once the plate-corslet was adopted there was no room for it. Homer mentions an obscure piece of armour worn somewhere near the waist, called the *mitrē*; some have identified this with a belt of the same type, others, less plausibly, with a semi-circular bronze plate which was sometimes suspended on rings at the lower edge of the corslet, and is found largely in Crete.[13] Later, experiments were made in adding supplementary pieces to the hoplite's panoply (see pp. 92–3), but these were temporary and optional features.

Well-protected as he was, the hoplite was far from invulnerable. As is shown by a number of dedications from Olympia, bronze plate-armour and shield-facings could both be pierced by the offensive weapons of the day; some of the holes in the armour are square, suggesting a thrust with the spear-butt (p. 80), which often had a square section. Nor was any adequate protection, at least in the early days, found for two vital spots, the throat and the groin. Although the later lengthening of the Corinthian helmet cheek-pieces (p. 93) must have done something for the throat, seventh-century vase-painters often show the phalanx, at the moment of joining battle, with their spears levelled at this point. The thrust at the groin below the shield is also often seen, and was perhaps used later in the action. Its results are described in a passage of Tyrtaeus (Frags. 6–7, lines 21–7), who attempts to shame his younger hoplites into resistance by painting a gruesome picture of a wounded older man. This was the kind of fighting for which the hoplite existed and, unlike the soldier in a modern bayonet charge, he had no long-range weapon (once the javelin had been abandoned) with which to 'soften up' the enemy first. In his close-packed phalanx he must have made a tempting target for the enemy missile-troops if there were a delay before battle was joined, and their fire, if seldom lethal, must have required constant alertness. Thereafter he could charge the enemy, but once the battle-lines met he had no further opportunity for swift movement—not even backwards, since the phalanx was at least four ranks deep. A phalanx battle, left to take its own course, allowed neither respite nor variety. Hoplite warfare required a steady nerve, and indeed, it is doubtful whether any other part-time, citizen army

34 Attic black-figure cup showing a giant throwing a javelin. The first two fingers of the throwing hand are hooked into a loop attached to the javelin shaft, giving much greater leverage to the cast. See p. 80.

35 Barbed bronze arrowhead, about 11 cm long, of a type that was for long associated with Crete. The Greeks generally wielded a bow made from a single stave, but a composite bow was used by the Cretan and Scythian mercenaries. Probably both types of bow could fire such arrows as this. See pp. 40, 81.

36 This relief-carved statue-base, showing warriors mounting a processional two-horse chariot, was found built into the city wall at Athens. Here, too, the charioteer is unarmed, reflecting the practice of the battles of the past. About 500 BC. See p. 87. *cf.* p. 71.

37 Attic black-figure amphora by Exekias (c. 540–530 BC). The two heroes Achilles and Ajax, equipped as hoplites, are playing a boardgame, their shields leaning against the wall behind them. The painting shows in detail the thigh and upper arm guards which formed an optional part of the hoplite's panoply. See p. 93.

has ever been set, as a matter of course, a more exacting task. It throws an interesting side-light on the background of many famous men in Greek history—not least, literary figures like Aeschylus, Socrates or Demosthenes—that they had been through this harsh school. *Pl. 26*

The swift and dramatic developments in the design of armour, which introduced the hoplite to Greek battlefields, were not matched by any immediate change in weapons. Indeed, in armour as well as weapons the years between approximately 700 and 650 seem to constitute a sort of transitional period. The bronze panoply of the hoplite was not, it seems, adopted universally or at once; for every warrior armed *cap-à-pie* there are several with only part of the equipment. Thus the warrior buried in the Argos grave had a hoplite corslet, but a primitive helmet, and as far as we know, neither shield nor greaves. The bronze figurines with Corinthian helmets have up-to-date headgear but no body-armour. On the vases, we often see men with a hoplite shield but no corslet; more rarely, the corslet with a pre-hoplite shield or no shield at all. These portrayals may not all be true to life, since Greek artists, at least in later days, could seldom resist showing as much of the human body as they could.[14] But offensive weapons give more decisive evidence of the transitional nature of the period. *Pl. 33*

The warrior of the Geometric period had fought with two or three spears, and used at least one as a javelin. The introduction of hoplite armour did not immediately affect this practice. Not only are the same types of iron spearhead retained in use, but the representations throughout the seventh century most often show hoplites with two spears.[15] It is true that they are seldom seen actually throwing them, but there are some more detailed pictures which show throwing-loops attached to the spear-shaft. This is a surprising state of affairs, since the single heavy thrusting-spear of the hoplite was to become the most characteristic of his attributes; to Aeschylus the Persian Wars are symbolized as the Spear against the Bow (*Persae* 813; cf. 280, 725, 1001-3). In action, the hoplite is usually shown in these early scenes thrusting with one spear, and holding the other in his left hand as a spare, which is curious. Possibly hoplites did for a time carry multiple spears, and only gradually realized that, with their shield and other equipment, these formed an excessive encumbrance; possibly the artists have misunderstood the purpose of the second spear. It is a measure of our ignorance that we cannot pronounce directly on such a basic question. So too with the sword: in the Classical period, the hoplite carried a short sword as a reserve weapon. He would not need it at all unless his spear had been broken or lost, and then he might need it in a hurry; a large blade would be unnecessary and indeed undesirable. But in the early vase-paintings we still see hoplites hewing at each other with swords of considerable length. There is every sign that the long iron sword characteristic of the Dark Age was still in use. The only real change is the very rare occurrence of a one-edged weapon, with a one-sided hilt;[16] this could be used only for a cutting stroke, and is the ancestor of the short slashing-sword which was to become prominent in Classical times (p. 97).

But in time, hoplite warfare passed beyond the period of experiment and variety. The best sign that the hoplite has finally 'arrived' is given by a small group of vases of the Late Proto-corinthian style, and particularly by the jug painted in poly-chrome technique known as the Chigi Vase. Its main scene shows two hoplite forces on the point of joining battle. The tactics are those of the phalanx, and in essentials the same as they remained for three centuries afterwards; the only discordant note is that each man still wields two spears. Otherwise the standard features are already present: the men fight in close-packed ranks; they advance and join battle in step, to the music of a piper; they balance their first spear for an overhand thrust; they are all equipped with Corinthian helmet, plate-corslet, greaves and hoplite shield. Probably they would have been carrying a short sword in real life, but the artist perhaps wanted to avoid encumbering his picture with more details than were strictly necessary.[17] Pl. 30

To the hoplite, his equipment became a source of pride, not only as a status-symbol to show that he belonged to the class which could afford it, but as the principal medium through which he served his city. At Athens, the young hoplite, on completing his training, was presented with shield and spear[18] but had to find the rest of his equipment at his own expense. His armaments were kept hanging on the walls of the living-room, where the chief threat to them was smoke from the fire. Some of the most powerful scenes in Greek vase-painting are those which show a nameless, sometimes doomed, hoplite taking down his shield, or his wife bringing him his helmet. Whether armour was often passed on from father to son or brother to brother is doubtful; this could have been regarded as an attempted evasion of the property-qualification and further, the need for an exact fit, especially with the Corinthian helmet but also with the corslet and even the shield, must have made it impossible in many cases. On the other hand, the sons of hoplites killed in action were armed at the state's expense.

The hoplite has not always been seen in the guise presented here, as a largely original creation of Archaic Greece, and there is still room for disagreement today. The deep-seated (and justifiable) tendency to seek in Near Eastern lands for the origin of new phenomena in early Greece has been applied in this case too, but with limited results. Certainly massed heavy infantry had long been in use among the Oriental kingdoms, but for the fundamental feature of hoplite armour, the use of beaten sheet bronze, it is hard to find precedents here. Again, an oral and literary tradition speaks of the early pre-eminence of Carian armourers (p. 65), but one can find no external support for it. One of the obstacles to this and other 'Oriental' theories is the fact that the Ionian Greeks were not apparently among the pioneers of hoplite armour in Greece. The large round shield of Assyria and Urartu recalls that of the Greek hoplite, and indeed it is in the grimly efficient infantryman on the Assyrian palace reliefs that we see the only even approximate prototype for the hoplite; but his operations, in the flat country of cavalryman and archer, or on the steep mountains farther north, never look like those of the phalanx. Instead we have looked, paradoxically, in just the opposite direction for the source of a fundamental part of the hoplite's armament—to barbarian Europe, where bronze body-armour had been used, no doubt in very different circumstances, for some time previously.

A more recent argument is that which would point to Mycenaean Greece for the hoplite's antecedents. The objections to this are less than conclusive (*cf.* pp. 41–2), so long as we concentrate on the single items of armour—corslet, greave, helmet—present at both periods in roughly similar form. But does the total picture, at any point in the Mycenaean age, really resemble that of hoplite Greece? For metal plate-corslets, we must now go back to the 'Palace period' of the fifteenth and fourteenth centuries, where the evidence suggests that they were worn by an élite force organized and equipped from the palaces, and mounted in pairs on chariots. There is not a sign of massed heavy infantry in the art of this period. Conversely, the Late Mycenaean period shows organized infantry forces in uniform equipment, but no heavy armour. The soldiers on the Warrior Vase and its associated monuments are in predominantly non-metal armour, and carry shields of obscure type; their battle-formation corresponds, not quite to the phalanx, but to that on a small group of representations (Etruscan as well as Greek) which belong to the period of transition to the true phalanx. It would be remarkable if any modern interpretation of this complex process were to hit on the exact truth; but I would suggest that, whether or not the Mycenaeans would have developed the hoplite if given the time and the prosperity to do so, in the event the tide ran against them, and it was left to their descendants, beginning the same task almost from scratch half a millennium later, to carry it to its conclusion.

THE SPREAD OF HOPLITE ARMOUR

Once introduced, the hoplite with his panoply long held an almost undisputed mastery of Greek warfare. Cavalry was seldom a real threat to him, chariots had long since disappeared from the battlefield, and light-armed troops with missiles could not challenge him so long as he maintained his formation and kept to ground that was suitable for it. Part of the reason for this was that, for most Greek states, hoplites were the only properly-trained troops until well on in the Classical period. Light-armed forces existed, but there was not the time, nor even perhaps the desire to train the landless and the poor to the high degree of efficiency required for really effective skirmishers. Even their equipment was not standardized, as is shown by Thucydides' description of the Athenians at the battle of Delium as late as 424 (IV, 94). Cavalry, though for rather different reasons (pp. 85–6), long remained equally ineffective and disorganized. Even at sea, warships were for a time equipped with a fighting-deck on which hoplites, serving as marines, could be massed. When two ships clashed, the result was a miniature land battle afloat, with the hoplites doing the main fighting and missile-troops lending support. All these factors put the more advanced states of Greece under some pressure to raise a hoplite army, a step which in turn proved far-reaching. The men might provide their own armour, but it was the state which had to maintain the muster-rolls, supervise training and ensure that the men and their equipment were kept in an adequate state of fitness. Although a citizen army might seem naturally entitled to the full rights of citizenship, this was not a notion easily accepted at this early date. When it was found necessary to extend the franchise to the hoplite class in order to ensure their dependability in warfare, the step was a fateful one. Aristotle commemorates it as the beginning of Greek democracy.[19]

It is hard for us today, with our preconceptions about staff-work and tactics, chains of command and officer-classes, to picture the working of a hoplite army to which, with the partial exception of Sparta, none of these factors applied. For a long time hoplites, however well trained, remained strictly amateurs in Greece itself, although service in foreign lands was another matter. In Plato's *Laches* (182 A–B) there is as good a picture as any of the somewhat condescending attitude of the classical Athenian to hoplite training. A hoplite force was socially homogeneous, and the phalanx was made up of smaller units, adopted from civilian life; its members served more or less indifferently as subordinate officers or privates, the possibilities of tactical initiative in a hoplite battle being small. Most Greek cities had

very few officers to a phalanx. Sparta went to the other extreme—
as Thucydides said, 'Almost all their army, except for a small
part, consists of officers under officers' (V, 66, 4). The end result
was probably not very different; it was not this which won
Sparta's battles for her. At a higher level, the generalship was
admittedly one of the most esteemed offices in the state, but it
was often held by men who were militarily almost novices, and
even here the possibilities of skilful decision were nearly exhausted
with the choosing of a battle-ground to suit the phalanx. Trickery
with signals was one of the few remaining resources, as at the
battle of Sepeia (Herodotus VI, 78). Here Cleomenes of Sparta,
noticing that his Argive enemies, encamped near by, were
closely observing his signals and acting on them themselves,
warned his men, when next they received the signal 'Dismiss
for dinner', to attack instead. The Argives were surprised and
routed as he had planned. Once battle was joined, the generals
too commonly fought as hoplites in the ranks; hence the remark-
ably high death-rate among them. *Pl. 54*

The widespread adoption of the hoplite was not only the
result of mutual pressure between cities. It exercised a peculiar
appeal in itself to Greek states, who were nearly always primarily
concerned with the protection of the crops on which they
depended for livelihood and ultimately survival. A single hoplite
battle at the frontier, fought in early summer, would usually give
a clear-cut result to a campaign, enabling the victors both to
exact terms from the defeated, on pain of destroying their crops,
and to return and attend to their own harvest. It was fitting that
the hoplites, themselves largely drawn from the class of farmers
and landowners, should have been the main participants in
this game of agricultural poker. The privileged position of the
Spartans, who did not have to do their own agricultural work,
enabled them to campaign at seasons disconcerting to the other
Greeks. But it was left to Alexander to introduce Greece to
systematic winter campaigning.

How far can the spread of the hoplite system be traced in our
records, written and material? The discovery of a single piece
of hoplite armour, or even of a whole panoply, in a particular

region of Greece need not imply very much in itself; any well-heeled soldier might take the trouble to protect himself with bronzearmrou on his own initiative. Nor does the appearance of hoplite figures in a city's art necessarily mean that the city had acquired a fully-fledged hoplite army, for such artistic motifs may be simply borrowed from other schools. But by amassing the different fragments of evidence, we can build up a fair picture of the style of warfare practised in many Greek city-states. As we should now expect, the ascendancy of hoplite armour spreads far and fast; but at the same time there is a marked growth in regionalism. A hoplite remained a hoplite provided that he had the necessary degree of protection and fought in a particular way; but this allowed for considerable local variations in the style of his various pieces of equipment, especially the helmet.

We may briefly consider the main military powers of the Aegean in turn. To begin with, there is no better example of regional deviation than that of the armour used in seventh-century Crete. The island was at that time enjoying a short-lived resurgence, artistic and cultural—a last reminder of her greatness in Minoan times, before she relapsed again into comparative obscurity. Hoplite armour is attested very early in Crete: there is a bronze relief showing Corinthian helmets which may date from before 700, and the earliest actual examples of the bronze greave known in the Aegean after the Bronze Age are also from Crete. The Cretans also had the practice, uncommon in mainland Greece, of dedicating miniature replicas of pieces of armour at their sanctuaries. From this evidence, we get an impression of typical Cretan individuality: the helmets look at first like Corinthian ones, but they have a rigidly horizontal lower edge, and lack the usual long nose-guards which all but a few Corinthian helmets possess; the Cretan corslets share the same general features as the 'bell' shape found at Argos, but they are longer and more severe in shape, making no apparent concessions to the contours of the body; the greaves are short and small, and must have required laces to keep them on.[20] The 'Insular' helmet (p. 52) may have been devised here. Then there is that peculiarly Cretan piece of armour, the semi-circular stomach-guard, today commonly called the *mitrē* (p. 56). The Cretans at this period often decorated their bronze armour with scenes, sometimes quite elaborate, in repoussé work; perhaps for this reason their products occasionally appear as dedications at the Greek sanctuary-sites, particularly Delphi. *Pl. 32*

Very different is the picture of Ionia, a term which in its loosest sense may be taken to include the whole western coast of Asia Minor and the offshore islands, from Lesbos in the north to Rhodes in the south. Here too there are regional adaptations; but East Greece as a whole, so far from being a cul-de-sac, is in constant touch with the rest of Greece, and indeed long serves as a bridge to the barbarian east. So fragmentary is the evidence that we cannot be sure when the hoplite panoply first reached this side of the Aegean. Around 650 BC, when Ionia was threatened by Cimmerian invaders from the interior, the Ephesian poet Callinus encouraged his fellow-citizens to resist, in a poem which unmistakably refers to javelin-throwing:

'And let each man throw his spear for the last time as he dies' (1, line 5).

and 'Often he will escape the carnage, and the sound of javelins...' (line 14).

This is perhaps a sign that here too, the period was at most one of transition in the style of warfare. But about two generations later, when the Lesbian poet Alcaeus describes his armour in detail, the hoplite panoply is evidently in general use:

'The great house gleams with bronze; the whole roof is [well?] decked with bright helmets, on which white horsehair crests nod from above, to adorn men's heads; bright bronze greaves hang on hidden pegs, a barrier against the strong missile; and corslets of new linen and hollow shields, thrown down; with them are Chalcidian swords, with them many belts and tunics. These we may not forget...' Frag. 54 (Diehl), Z 34 (Lobel and Page).

Apart from the linen corslets (see p. 90) and the belts which go naturally with them, this is standard hoplite equipment, though the spear, curiously enough, is absent.

The two sanctuaries of Hera on Samos and Athena at Lindos have yielded specimens of armour, but these are often of unorthodox type. Representations are more helpful: from Samos comes a series of miniature shields which are shaped like hoplite ones, and a vase in the shape of a head wearing a Corinthian helmet; these are of early date, not very long after 700.[21] More important is a literary tradition: in about 664 the Egyptian Psamtik or Psammetichos led a movement to unify his country after the Assyrian occupation had ended, and made himself the first Pharaoh of the XXVI Dynasty. From Herodotus and other writers we learn that he was helped by mercenaries from Ionia and Caria, and that the arrival of these men in their bronze armour fulfilled a prophecy made to him, that he should win the aid of Brazen Men. These soldiers, whose appearance was so portentous and whose military aid decisive, can only have been hoplites. It is noteworthy that the Ionian Greeks were joined in this enterprise by the Carians—a non-Greek people, but one that was soon to become Hellenized, and had evidently already adopted the panoply. The Carians were indeed credited by many Greek writers with having invented certain elements of the hoplite's equipment, but more probably they simply popularized them by their long and widespread service as mercenary hoplites.[22]

Somewhat before 600, the eastern Greeks made a contribution to the development of armour by devising a kind of helmet, clearly based on the Corinthian but more elaborate. It varies considerably in detail, but the regular features are a flat, semi-circular piece guarding the forehead, with an ornamental projection above; a spreading, sharply-offset neck-guard at the back; and cheek-pieces which are made separately and sometimes hinged at the level of the temple. No complete example has been found, and the best evidence is provided by the very common little clay flasks (*aryballoi*) in the shape of a helmeted head. The helmet is almost always of this type, and the fabric and distribution of these vases confirm the Ionian origin of their model. If one had to choose a single place for its invention, Rhodes would perhaps be the likeliest guess. The Ionian helmet is portrayed over a wide range within Greece, and there are representations of it from Phrygia and Phoenicia which suggest that, to these Oriental peoples, it was the Ionian version of the Greek hoplite which was most familiar.[23] Some of the eastern peoples, besides the Carians, went so far as to adopt hoplite armour themselves: Herodotus tells us that in 480 the troops from Lydia, Pamphylia and Cyprus serving in Xerxes' host had equipment very close to that of the Greeks (VII, 74, 90). Cyprus has indeed produced examples of the Corinthian helmet and the hoplite shield-band reliefs (cf. p. 54). *Pls. 25, 47*

On the mainland of Greece, the evidence is variable—quite full for some states, almost non-existent for others. But the overall picture is a fairly homogeneous one in the early stages. We may begin with the Peloponnese; the best-documented areas are also perhaps the three dominant military powers in seventh-century Greece, Sparta, Argos and Corinth. For Sparta, the verses attributed to the warrior-poet Tyrtaeus give a vivid picture of warfare in the mid-century. The people of Messenia, subdued by the Spartans some time earlier, had revolted, and only after a prolonged struggle did Sparta crush them. Several of Tyrtaeus' surviving poems are encouragements to the city's hoplite army, which is armed with corslet, round hoplite shield, spear and sword:

'Those who dare to go forward, shoulder to shoulder, into the mêlée, into the van, die in less numbers, and save their people behind them' (Frag. 8, line 11).
'Let each man learn to fight by doing brave deeds, and not stand with his shield, out of range of the missiles' (line 27).
'. . . and standing foot to foot, shield pressed on shield, crest to crest and helmet to helmet, chest to chest engage your man, grasping your sword-hilt or long spear' (line 31).

This is evidently propaganda for the tactics of the phalanx, still at the most in process of introduction, for the hoplites are still operating in close combination with the *gumnetes*—the 'naked men' or light-armed troops:

'And you for your part, light-armed, crouch under your shields' (or perhaps, 'under the *hoplites'* shields') 'on each side, and hurl your great stones or cast your smooth javelins at them, keeping your position close to the hoplites' (line 35).

It does seem that the formation of the army in Tyrtaeus is loose and even disorganized.[24]

For early Sparta there is another kind of evidence in the shape of small, mass-produced lead relief-figurines of hoplites, cast from a roughly-finished mould, which have been found in large quantities in and near Sparta. It is unlikely that any of these are quite as early as Tyrtaeus and his war, but thereafter they continue to be produced for centuries, sometimes using the old moulds. The emblems on the shields are purely decorative—rosettes, circles, catherine-wheel patterns and the like—although by the fifth century the Spartan army had adopted as its shield-device the letter Λ (the initial of Lacedaemon). In the same way the men of Messenia adopted a M and the Sicyonians Σ, while the Thebans used a club (the attribute of their city's patron Heracles) and the Mantineans a trident. In some cases these devices were applied to coins as well as shields.[25] Because of the decline of Spartan art in and after the Archaic period, we have few contemporary illustrations of the great days of Spartan infantry, but we have at least a glimpse of the beginning of the process by which, without any superiority of equipment, the hoplites of Sparta became supreme on the battlefield, and among the most feared troops in the world.

In the seventh century, however, the cities of Argos and Corinth were probably at least as powerful militarily as Sparta. Both almost certainly played an important part in the development of the hoplite panoply. It would be hard to prove this by archaeological evidence alone, but by the fifth century and probably well before, the standard shield and helmet of the hoplite were called Argive and Corinthian respectively. In art, it is often hard to distinguish Argive style from Corinthian, but the scenes on the hoplite shield-bands (p. 54) find their best artistic parallels in Argos, while the standard rim-decorations for both shields and helmets can certainly be associated with the north-eastern Peloponnese generally.[26] Further, it was at Argos that the very earliest examples of metal helmet and corslet in Iron Age Greece were found. For Corinth, on the other hand, we have the secure testimony of pottery: a whole series of scenes, mostly painted on tiny aryballoi and extending over much of the seventh century, shows hoplite armour either being worn in action or, more rarely, in still life arrangements—a sign that hoplite warfare had become one of the main preoccupations of the times. An aryballos of around 700 gives us the earliest painted representation of the Corinthian helmet, together with more obscure objects which, I believe, represent the arm-band and blazon of the hoplite's shield—three of the bronzesmith's main contributions to the new panoply. Later, around the middle of the seventh century, Corinthian artists give the lead in showing troops operating in formation, as a phalanx—a new theme which suggests a subject of recent appearance. On the Chigi Vase is the culmination of this school of military art, a battle-scene so elaborate that it may well have been inspired by a large-scale painting (p. 58). The use of a piper, as shown here, to take the men into action instead of the more usual trumpeter, was a practice which the Spartans also adopted now or later. A trumpet or other signalling-device was, incidentally, an essential requirement for the handling of hoplites in battle; we read in Greek literature of distinct trumpet-calls for at least the basic manoeuvres of 'charge' and 'retire'. It has recently been suggested that Cleon's disaster at Amphipolis (Thucydides V, 10; pp. 54, 105) was the result of a mishandling of signalling practices.[27] Pl. 30

The seventh-century Corinthian vase-paintings, from our point of view, represent the high-water mark of this kind of evidence. Later Greek taste inclined more and more towards heroic battle-scenes, in which not only the participants, but also their equipment and style of combat, were sometimes taken from tradition or from the artist's imagination. By the time of the Persian Wars at the latest, we know that hoplite armies had grown up in a number of the lesser cities of the north-eastern Peloponnese who involuntarily fell in the sphere of influence, more or less direct, of Corinth and Argos: such as Megara and Sicyon, Troezen and Epidaurus, as well as Corinthian colonies like Potidaea, Ambracia and Corcyra. Artistic or archaeological evidence is largely wanting for these cities.[28]

During the seventh century Athens, later a leader in so many fields, was apparently content to follow in the development of armour. Painted vases show her soldiers adopting the corslet, greaves, Corinthian helmet and Argive shield in their orthodox form. According to some very late sources, Athens became famous for her production of corslets, and certainly in 412 she was able to equip 1,500 Argives as hoplites in addition to her own large force. By the sixth century we find Athenian originality asserting itself with the development of the 'Attic' helmet.[29] The name is a modern one, but it is probably justified. It is given to a kind of head-piece regularly shown in representations of Athena on Attic vases from the first half of the sixth century onwards. A light, open type of helmet which covers neither forehead, cheeks nor ears, it is sometimes little more than a skull-cap with a crest, but more often there is a neck-guard on the model of the Ionian helmet, and a kind of frontlet standing up above the forehead like a tiara, usually terminating on each side with a volute, near the ear; sometimes there are hinged cheek-pieces, too. One might wonder whether this helmet was a perquisite of Athena, but human warriors wear it as well in Attic art, and it is also regularly given to Amazons, from at least as early a date as to Athena. Surviving examples are extremely rare.

At the same time another variety of helmet should be mentioned, since it too appears in the early sixth century and is prominent at Athens. It is usually given the name 'Chalcidian', for the obscure reason that it appears on the pottery which today bears this name among archaeologists—most conspicuously, on a vase in Berlin with two large-scale helmeted heads facing each other, in a panel on either side of the vase. On one side both helmets are Corinthian; on the other, one head wears the Corinthian and one this new type—a theme which seems designed to draw attention to the second, much rarer variety. This 'Chalcidian' black-figured pottery is found in Italy and Sicily, mostly in Etruria and in the colonies planted in the West by the Euboean city of Chalcis: hence the name. Since the distribution of the actual examples of this kind of helmet is also weighted towards southern Italy, it is possible that, just as the pottery is now often derived from this area, so the helmet might be an original contribution of the western Greeks. Nevertheless, it is probably commonest in Attic art, and Athena herself sometimes wears it.[30] The remote link with Euboean Chalcis is valuable chiefly as a warning against accepting such local names too readily. This helmet is no more than a variant of the Corinthian type in any case. It looks like a systematic attempt to soften it down; instead of the sharp jutting cheek-pieces it has rounded ones, which are often developed decoratively into the shape of a ram's head in relief; a special aperture is introduced at the sides so as to leave the ears free, thus curing what must have been a serious defect of the Corinthian type. What brings it closest to the Attic helmet is the use of relief spirals and wavy lines on the temple and forehead; many modern publications run the two types together into one. The finest surviving Greek helmet, the bronze example with its superb towering ram's head crowned by a silver crest, in the City Art Museum St. Louis, belongs most nearly to the Chalcidian type.[31] *Pl. 24*

In the island of Euboea, the two leading cities, Chalcis and Eretria, both claimed a great military past. There was a tradition that men of Euboea first devised the bronze panoply of the hoplite, and it is a fact that Chalcis became the outstanding centre of production of iron swords in Greece, as Toledo did of steel in medieval Europe.[32] Of these achievements, archaeology has found sadly little trace, largely because the exploration of the sites, and particularly that of the Classical levels at Chalcis, has been less than thorough. There is no early armour from Euboea; we cannot point to a single Chalcidian sword; and as we have seen the association of the 'Chalcidian' helmet with Chalcis is at best tenuous. Euboeans were certainly prominent among the

Greeks who used the early trading-post at Al Mina, at the mouth of the Orontes, from the late ninth century onwards, but it is highly questionable whether they could have brought from here the specific inventions ascribed to Euboea, the bronze shield and the plate-corslet. At present, therefore, even if we substitute borrowing for invention, there seems little support for the literary tradition; but we may readily accept some equally old, if vaguer, traditions about Euboean warriors. In Homer they are mentioned as 'spearmen eager to rend the corslets on the chests of enemies'; Archilochus, a contemporary of the events of the first half of the seventh century, records that the lords of Euboea, famous spearmen, are also skilled in the sword-battle; while an anonymous verse, perhaps of similar date, begins by calling the men of Chalcis the finest in Greece, although it goes on to prefer the 'linen-corsleted Argives'—perhaps a sign of later manipulation of the text. We also know that sixty chariots took part in a ceremonial procession at an annual festival near Eretria; if a genuine trace of the use of the chariot in warfare, this must derive from a very early period indeed.[33] Euboean colonies, especially those of Chalcidice in the north-western Aegean, grew to be substantial hoplite powers.

The remainder of Greece seems to have lagged behind the cities we have been discussing in the field of warfare. A partial exception is Arcadia, which, for all its proverbial pastoralism, was a formidable source of hoplites. The city of Tegea in particular is known for her long and by no means unsuccessful struggle against Spartan aggression in the sixth century, and for the heroism of her hoplites at Plataea in 479. Orchomenus and Mantinea could also command a well-armed force, and Arcadians in general became the outstanding hoplite mercenaries in the late fifth century. But again, archaeological finds bear little witness to this; a few hoplite shield-bands, and two finds of greaves from the mountainous fringes of Arcadia, one from a probably sixth-century grave, the other an inscribed dedication of the fifth century, are almost all the armour that we have from Arcadian sites. But the sanctuary of Apollo at Bassae produced miniature armour which curiously resembles the Cretan finds (pp. 52, 63), not only in conception but in detail.[34] This is also an apposite moment to remember that the greater sanctuaries of Greece attracted offerings from all over the country and beyond, and that the greatest of them, Olympia, lies not far outside Arcadian territory and has certainly produced other finds of Arcadian workmanship. Except in the rare case of inscribed pieces, we shall probably never know the ultimate source of much of the armour dedicated at a site like Olympia, but there is reason to think that the nearer parts of Greece, not least the territory of Elis which surrounded Olympia, contributed at least a proportionate part. In later days Elis had a hoplite army, though one of no great repute; she was a rich state by Greek standards, and Polybius in a still later age suggested that she would have done better to sit back and employ mercenaries for her defence.[35]

A different and interesting case is provided by the northern-most region of the Peloponnese, Achaea, which, except in the latest Mycenaean period and again in Hellenistic times, seems to have been somewhat backward. Hoplite armour was known here, for in a seventh-century pithos-burial on the Achaean-Arcadian border were found an 'Illyrian' helmet of early type and a pair of greaves of rather stubby shape, which might be local products, besides a sword and three spears; an even earlier Corinthian helmet has been found in Patras.[36] Yet our historical sources allege that, when the Achaean cities had formed a league and furnished a joint army in the Hellenistic period, that army was still equipped with small spears and oblong shields until the general Philopoemen introduced the equipment and tactics of the phalanx—probably the Macedonian phalanx—with con-spicuously successful results (see p. 127). This is an astonishingly late development (it belongs to the years 208 and following), and as a matter of fact the tradition as here presented cannot be quite accurate, since we read of 'hoplites' and 'cuirassiers' in Achaean armies before Philopoemen (e.g. Xenophon, *Anabasis* VI, 2, 10; Polybius IV, 12, 3; 14, 6); but it was probably true that the hoplite had been, for nearly five hundred years, a less than regular feature of Achaean armies. The same was no doubt

38 Attic black-figure amphora showing Greek hoplites fighting alongside Scythian mercenary archers. The hoplites carry their usual equipment, including the heavy shield behind which the archers, lightly armed apart from their composite bows, could shelter. Late sixth century BC. See pp. 83-4.

39 Funerary stele commemorating an Athenian warrior named Aristion, who died, apparently in battle, not long before the time of Marathon. He is wearing the composite cuirass which replaced the earlier 'bell' corslet; his small helmet may originally have been of the Corinthian type before the breakage and subsequent trimming of the top of the stele. See pp. 91, 94, 142.

40-41 *Above, right:* Attic red-figure plate of about 515 BC with an inscription to Miltiades, showing a mounted archer in Scythian dress, armed with a composite bow. He is wearing a leather cap and what may be quilted garments, but no metal body-armour. See pp. 82-3. *Below, right:* Black-figure *mastos* cup showing mounted hoplites, who will dismount to fight. The absence of stirrups and horseshoes made the cavalry a much less effective arm in Classical times than later. About 530 BC. See p. 85.

42-44 Details of a red-figure volute-krater showing Greeks fighting Amazons. The two Greeks are wearing respectively a laced composite corslet (*left*) and two comparative innovations, the Thracian helmet and the plated 'muscle' cuirass (*below, left*). This last type of armour required very careful fitting to the measurements of the individual owner. The Amazon (*below, right*) has a scaled corslet and a short slashing sword, used with an overhand stroke. About 470 BC. See pp. 90-1, 92, 95, 97.

true of other remoter areas of Greece: an example is Opuntian Locris, across the Gulf of Corinth, where a somewhat later warrior was buried with his Corinthian helmet and a whole armoury of weapons, in the sixth century.[37] The discovery of such stray survivals of the practice of burial with arms, at a time when most Greeks had abandoned it permanently, is of great value.

The majority of the cities and regions of Greece remain un-accounted for, and they include some major centres: Thebes, for instance, and the other cities of Boeotia, where fine hoplite armies came into existence and where a particular kind of helmet was devised (see p. 94) not later than the Persian Wars. A few shield-band reliefs from Boeotia, and two shields from Olympia inscribed in Boeotian characters as booty from the men of Tanagra, are all that we have. Aegina too, though an important hoplite and naval power, preserves an almost complete anonymity in this as in some other fields of Greek archaeology. Other fragments of evidence of various kinds are scattered thinly over the Aegean and Ionian islands. Archilochus of Paros probably fought with a shield of hoplite type (p. 53). Naxos boasted 8000 hoplites in about 500 BC; excavations on Siphnos have revealed terracotta miniature shields, datable soon after 700, which look as though they are of hoplite type: a sanctuary on the island of Ithaca produced a greave, and the suggestion of hoplites in this area is strengthened by the fact that the neighbouring islands of Leucas and Cephallenia furnished small forces of hoplites at Plataea in 479, and Zakynthos a larger one in 432. Beyond this we may imagine a few regions where the heavy-armed hoplite and the set-piece battle remained unaccepted; sometimes, no doubt, in areas of very rough terrain, wisely so. The prime example is Aetolia, for whose arms and methods there is evidence from the time of the Peloponnesian War (p. 105). But even in an Aetolian sanctuary, dedications of hoplite shield-bands are known, a relic perhaps of Corinthian penetration.[38]

The evidence for hoplite warfare in Greece is thus thinly spread, and the resultant picture a shadowy one. We shall look in vain for accounts of early battles to illustrate the developments here described. Some inkling, it is true, of the prowess of hoplites in relation to foreign troops is already given by events such as the Psammetichos incident (p. 65) and the distinguished service of Alcaeus' brother, Antimenidas, in the Babylonian army about seventy years later (p. 77). Modern historians have at times gone further, and inferred the agency of hoplites in military, and indeed political, events of seventh-century Greece—such as the decisive victory of the Argives over Sparta at Hysiae, dated to 669 BC by the much later Pausanias, and the seizure of power by the first Corinthian tyrant, Cypselus, not many years later. Such conclusions, however acutely argued, must remain little more than informed guesses, unless new evidence comes to light. Yet, fortunately, the one quite certain conclusion is in many ways the most significant and surprising of all: that hoplites had already begun to appear by the late eighth century, and a phalanx formation organized at least by the middle of the seventh. In other words, the hoplite and his tactics were already about 200 years old at the time when we first see, in any detail, their vindication in action. The Persian Wars thus provide one of history's rare instances of a long-entrenched school of warfare being confronted with a new enemy, with unfamiliar and hitherto very effective methods, and triumphing over him.

Fortunately, also, some independent light is thrown on this vital period by the comparable experience of Italy. The prowess of the hoplite and his equipment were too great to be confined to Greece, and we have already seen (p. 66) that hoplite warfare was actually adopted by some of the non-Greek peoples of the East. It is less surprising to find it spreading to Italy and Sicily, where Greek colonies were numerous and powerful. For the purely Greek cities and sanctuaries there, our evidence is curiously defective: scarcely any armour and comparatively few weapons have come to light in them, and what there is seems to be as often of Italic as of Greek manufacture. No doubt the hoplite armies of Greek Italy were real enough, but literary sources tend to emphasize other arms; at Cumae, where in 524, if only we could believe the account of the battle by Dionysius of Halicarnassus (VII, 3–4), the city's cavalry were largely responsible for the most remarkable feat of arms in Greek warfare, when they routed (with some use of natural aids) an Etruscan and allied force which outnumbered them by more than a hundred to one. There are, however, several dedications from western Greek cities among the finds at Olympia, and we can infer the agency of the western Greeks with confidence at other points—for example, in a small group of curiously misshapen Corinthian helmets found in Italy, some of them composed of two horizontally-divided halves. This strange expedient again testifies to the difficulty of beating out such a helmet in one piece.[39] But by the late seventh century, or very soon afterwards, the Greeks of Italy must have partaken in a far-reaching event, the transmission of the hoplite panoply to the Etruscans, and perhaps other Italian peoples.

The richness of Etruscan art and grave-finds gives an unequalled picture of the adoption of hoplite armour, though at times in slightly idiosyncratic forms. Previously, Etruscan warriors had fought with medium-sized round shields, faced with bronze, and worn the splendid crested helmets and other types which their Villanovan predecessors had imported from the Urnfield peoples farther north; they may even have had the ornate bronze corslets (p. 41) which came from the same barbarian source. They were thus vastly better equipped than pre-hoplite Greece had been, yet the appearance of Greek hoplites on their shores was enough to launch a full-scale military reform in Etruria. It may have begun in the later seventh century—an actual example of a Greek or Grecian-style hoplite shield of this time was found near Fabriano, inland from Ancona—but by the middle of the sixth century it had apparently affected the armies of most of the main Etruscan cities. We should not imagine that the regular phalanx, or even the regular panoply, were adopted all at once in Etruria. Many of the representations show men with unorthodox weapons or deficient armour, the greave, for example, being absent in the earliest scenes. The tactics of the phalanx ultimately, however, won acceptance in Etruria; this we know from Roman sources. Probably before 500, the growing ambitions of Rome and her prolonged struggle with Etruria led her armies to copy the example of her powerful neighbours, and fight 'with bronze shield and by phalanx'. Thus, at a surprisingly early date, falls the first case of the influence, albeit indirect, of Greek arms on Roman—a process that was to be renewed three centuries later when the two powers came into direct confrontation. Even now, Greek and Italian were occasionally fighting side by side: at Aricia, just before 500, it was her Cumaean allies—hoplites most probably—who played the major part in saving the city from the Etruscans under Aruns (Dionysius VII, 5–6). Two centuries later we even find a Greek, Agathocles of Syracuse, hiring Etruscan mercenaries (again, probably hoplites); and incidentally massacring them, perhaps to avoid having to pay them—one of the hazards that mercenaries have sometimes had to face. We may assume that many of the Italic peoples farther south had also adopted hoplite armour; here too the finds on native sites continue to outnumber those from Greek ones.[40] Until the fourth century, it seems that Rome was using the hoplite as her main instrument of expansion in this and other parts of Italy. *Pl. 31*

But the notion of the hoplite was one which Greece passed on far beyond the limits of her colonization or even, perhaps, of direct trade. We find the items of the panoply being imported or imitated in many quite remote areas of Europe. There are corslets of a pattern closely modelled on the Greek 'bell' shape from Carinthia at the eastern end of the Alps, with an outlying example in central France. There are 'Illyrian' helmets, whose workmanship in some cases stamps them as direct Greek imports, not only from the area which gave the type its misleading name, but from Bosnia, Serbia and Rumania. There is a group of 'bell' corslets from Bulgaria, decidedly archaic in appearance but in fact dating from as late as the fifth century. There are two fine Corinthian helmets from Spain, one of them extremely early.[41] In the other direction, there is a fragment of a sixth-century shield from Persepolis in Iran—this perhaps looted from the conquered Ionian Greeks. There is a bronze greave, and the remains of an unusual kind of shield, not hoplite but demonstrably Greek, from Carchemish in north Syria, which were probably used by mercenaries in a siege of 604 BC. If artistic representations can be relied on, Phrygia was familiar with the hoplite in the sixth century, and the other barbarian neighbours of the Ionian Greeks were certainly fighting in hoplite armour (p. 66). The poet Alcaeus' brother Antimenidas enlisted, presumably as a mercenary hoplite, in the service of King Nebuchadnezzar of Babylon, and in a campaign perhaps belonging to the year 594 killed a giant enemy champion in single combat. An inscription was scratched on the leg of a statue at Abu Simbel, far up the Nile, by Greek mercenaries taking part in an expedition in about 590; these were probably hoplites, like their predecessors who came to help Psamtik I two generations earlier[42] (p. 65). The Greeks would not have liked it, but the fact was that to many barbarians their most valued contribution to the development of culture was the bronze armour of the hoplite.

OTHER ARMS

The hoplite has engaged much of our attention, both for his historical pre-eminence and because his equipment was so much more extensive, and less perishable, than that of other troops. But the arms of other Greek soldiers before the Persian Wars must now be considered. They did not always differ from those of the hoplite: sword and spear, for instance, were used by light-armed infantry and cavalry as well. But there were other aspects of Greek warfare—archery is the prime example—which required equipment and skill entirely different from the hoplite's. Our ignorance of much of the military field should not be under-estimated: there is still room for learned discussion, and complete disagreement, over many fundamental questions, such as whether or not the Athenian 'cavalryman' of the seventh, sixth and early fifth centuries actually rode his horse into battle; and what the dominant type of warship of Classical Greece, the trireme, actually looked like and how it worked.

To take first the other forms of infantry; since a hoplite was normally required to provide his very elaborate equipment at his own expense, it follows that the great mass of people in any Greek state could not afford to fight as hoplites. In a naval power like fifth-century Athens, many of them might serve as rowers in the fleet, but this situation was neither typical nor permanent; and even in Athens the light-armed troops could be as numerous as the hoplites, though it was long before they were regularly armed. Elsewhere, there were many cities that had no significant fleet, and many other regions which, as we have seen, either lacked the resources and expertise for equipping a hoplite army, or for geographical reasons preferred other forms of warfare. The light-armed infantryman was thus a common, if not yet very effective, feature of Greek armies and battlefields. How was he equipped?

The time-honoured function of the light-armed soldiers in Greece was to serve as javelin-throwers (*akontistai*). The more specialized services of the slinger and archer may be treated separately, and were in any case often performed by professional mercenaries. The javelin-thrower, like the hoplite, had come by the fifth century to take his name from his shield; he is usually described as a *peltastes*, from the *pelta* which he carried. This was invariably made of impermanent materials, normally wicker-work faced with animal-skin; we rely, therefore, on vase-paintings for our knowledge of its appearance. It was regarded as a characteristically Thracian arm. As we know from Aristotle, it was covered in goat's or sheep's hide, with no rim or facing. Although we sometimes see it carried by Thracian, Scythian or Greek light-armed troops, many of the best pictures on Attic vases show it in the hands of Amazons, who were often given foreign or unusual equipment. In its most distinctive form it was shaped like a broad crescent, normally held sideways, with the tips uppermost, but the identification so often made between this crescent-shape and the *pelta* is by no means universally valid, as is shown by a number of ancient references to different-shaped *peltai*, some of them simply round. Indeed, there is awkwardly enough a note in the second-century AD Greek lexicographer Phrynichus of Bithynia, that the wicker-work shields 'such as Amazons carry in paintings' are called *gerrha*; the *gerrhon* is known elsewhere as a Persian shield (p. 101).[43] The two terms may have become confused; but in any case Amazons in art are not generally given a shield in any way distinctive before the mid-sixth century. We may conclude that at this period the use of the *pelta*, spreading from Thrace, became familiar in Athens; perhaps as a result of the tyrant Pisistratus' having recruited mercenaries from Paeonia, a region not far from Thrace, during a period of exile.[44] But if so, it was more than a century before the Greek cities themselves began to organize properly-armed peltast forces (see pp. 98, 110).

Before Pisistratus, light troops must have carried a shield, perhaps under a different name. There are glimpses in art and literature to show what such a shield was like, but we cannot point to a surviving example that could be called typical. From our evidence we should certainly conclude that it was round, which makes it difficult to differentiate in art from the hoplite shield. The best indication is when the shield is shown held by the hand only, with the full length of the arm extended. Such shields are usually shown either as strongly convex, or with a projection in the middle; they vary greatly in size, and can be very small indeed, which would be no disadvantage if they were to be used as mobile parrying-shields, and on occasion even for an offensive jab, like the spiked targes of the Highlanders. They must have been commonly made of perishable material. There are bronze-faced shields with projecting centres found in Greece, but they are mostly of exotic, non-Greek shapes, which we look for largely in vain in Greek art. More prominent is a simpler form, with a central boss or bulge and often a decoration in concentric circles. Shortly before the appearance of the *pelta* in Greece, the black-figure painter, Lydos, shows an Amazon holding a shield with a spiked boss akin to this type.[45]

Light-armed troops, by definition, did not normally wear body-armour; we may therefore turn to their weapons. Tyrtaeus (pp. 66-7) is our earliest witness for the use of organized light-armed troops, and it is probable that they were first used as a tactical force by Sparta. The javelin, their prime weapon, is not easily identified among surviving examples of spearheads; while the limited field of the vase-painter made it difficult for him to show one in flight. Occasionally, however, he was able to show the characteristic throwing-loop at about the centre-point of the shaft, which must greatly have increased the javelin's range. The index and second fingers were engaged in the loop, while the shaft was gripped by the rest of the hand. Some actual spear-heads are so small that they can only have served for javelins, but small size, though an advantage, is hardly so important for a javelin as balance.[46] This could best be achieved by giving the head a slim blade and a long hollow socket, so as to shift the centre of gravity backwards—a method exemplified by the later Roman *pilum*. But perhaps the best indication of all, as in the Dark Age (p. 38), is given when multiple spears are used. Warrior graves in the period after this are no longer common, but there are one or two examples in outlying parts of Greece. In the seventh-century Achaean tomb which contained greaves and a helmet (p. 72) there were three spearheads of different lengths; in the rather later Locrian grave were two, with a spear-butt (*sauroter*) no less than seventeen inches long. In each case we may perhaps assume that the smaller heads were used as javelins; but if this is correct, the finds show that the javelin is not distinguished in its form, except by its somewhat narrower blade. The spear-butt in the Locrian grave must have been attached to the base of the larger spear. This weapon acquired great popularity in the hoplite period, and was apparently used by peltasts too. Unlike the spearhead, it was frequently made of bronze, perhaps because it was less necessary that it should be sharp, than that it should resist corrosion when the spear was stuck into the ground. It was commonly cast in a four-sided mould, giving a square section; often it had decorative mouldings, and occasionally examples captured from an enemy were inscribed before dedication. It helped to balance the weight of the iron spearhead, and served as a useful ancillary weapon in an emergency. Other more primitive weapons remained in use, such as the stone (pp. 40, 67) and the club, which we read of as carried by the bodyguards of Lesbian aristocrats and Athenian tyrants.[47]

We now come to the more specialized functions of the light-armed troops, among which archery takes first place. The Greeks did not pride themselves on their skill at archery, and there are numerous derogatory references to the bow, as an alien and somewhat effeminate weapon, in their literature. If we had to rely on literary evidence only, we should conclude that, Crete excepted, archery was almost unknown in Greece in the Archaic period, and that its introduction was then entirely brought about by the arrival of Scyths and Persians in the Aegean. But excavation has shown that this cannot be so. Crete is a different matter: representations of archers and finds of arrowheads continue to occur as they had in the Dark Age. The distinctively Cretan type of bronze tanged arrowhead (p. 40) is now found over a wide area—too wide, perhaps, for it to indicate the presence of Cretan archers in every case; in Samos was found a mould for casting these large arrowheads. Similarly, the type of composite bow which is recognizable only by its reflexed tips, and which we have associated with Crete, is occasionally shown in mainland art from the eighth century on. Cretan mercenary archers became, by the fifth century and even by the eighth and seventh, if we can trust Pausanias' anecdotes of the First and Second Messenian Wars, a familiar sight on Greek battlefields.[48] *Pl. 35*

But the native Greek aversion to archery must also have been overcome, and indeed the Attic Geometric vase-paintings suggest that this had happened before 700 (p. 40). Thereafter, the representations become increasingly untrustworthy, generally showing the bow in the hands of gods, heroes or Amazons. But this is offset by the finds of arrowheads in the Greek sanctuaries. These are often very numerous; sometimes they have a stratigraphical context which dates them well back in the Archaic period. At the siege of Smyrna in about 600, both the Lydian attackers and the Greek defenders shot arrows at each other, while a deposit of over eighty arrowheads at Lindos must date from before 525. It is noticeable that everywhere bronze predominates heavily over iron as the material, almost certainly because it lent itself so well to mass-production by casting. Other finds of the Archaic period have occurred at Sparta, Olympia and Perachora near the Isthmus of Corinth; on the islands of Chios and Delos; and at the Greek settlements in Cyrene, Egypt, Syria and Cyprus.[49]

This last group of finds points in a new direction, towards the great archer-peoples of the Orient. The bow had long been an established weapon in the Near and Middle East, but archery was revolutionized there by the arrival of successive waves of invaders from north of the Black Sea—the Cimmerians and Scyths. These peoples, long schooled in bowmanship either mounted or on foot, used a new form of both bow and arrows. The bow is the famous double-curved 'Cupid's Bow', familiar from the art of many ages since.[50] It acquires the distinctive 'Cupid's' shape when in the act of being drawn; when strung but not drawn (as for example when kept in the special combined bow-case and quiver, the *gorytos*, which the Scyths carried), it has a different but no less recognizable form, the undulating curve of the bow itself crossing and re-crossing the string. This makes the type difficult to mistake. But more useful archaeologically are the accompanying forms of arrowhead. These are tiny (seldom much over an inch long), cast in bronze with a hollow socket. They could only be fitted with a very slim shaft, usually a reed or a specially whittled yew twig, on average about eighteen inches in length. But the *gorytos* could hold from two to three hundred of these little arrows, as Scythian graves show, and their effectiveness is amply attested. All over Asia Minor, Syria, Palestine and other parts of the Near East these arrowheads are spread like sea-shells after an inundation. Their earliest appearances, which we may connect with the original invasions, are invariably in the seventh century, but they continue to appear long after the invaders were gone, a sign that they had been adopted by their erstwhile victims. Ultimately they spread right across Europe to the Atlantic.[51]

In the Aegean area, the bulk of the arrowheads of Archaic date are of this type, although there is little likelihood of Scythian mercenaries before the later sixth century, and none whatever of Scythian invaders. Greek artists begin to show the Scythian bow from the mid-seventh century on; one of its first appearances is in the hands of the goddess Artemis, but it later becomes the special weapon of Heracles.[52] We may doubt whether the Greeks themselves had yet mastered the use of the composite and highly flexible Scythian bow. Such a bow, to judge by more recent analogies, took months, perhaps years to make, and even to string it was a skilled art; we read in Herodotus that the Medes had to be specially instructed by Scythians in its use (I, 73, 3). The Scyths used a quite different hold for drawing back the arrow, gripping it between the first and second fingers of the right hand while the third and fourth held the string, and probably balancing the arrow on the left hand to the left of, or *inside*, the bow itself. This required some protection, usually an arm-guard, for the left wrist, but such guards are not seen in Greece, and the standard Greek practice was apparently to hold the arrow in a simple thumb-and-forefinger grip of the right hand and to release it to the right of, or *outside*, the bow. The flexible Scythian bow could also be drawn to the ear or even the right shoulder (given an arrow sufficiently long), in contrast to the normal Greek draw to the breast only. *Pl. 40*

Some years later occurred an interesting episode which we know almost exclusively from Attic vase-painting.[53] From about 530 to 500 the artists take up, quite intensively, the subject of the Scythian archer, a figure sometimes distinguished by barbarian facial features in addition to his trousered costume. There are several themes running through the paintings: we see the Scyths occupied with their traditional skills—testing arrows, stringing bows, tending horses; occasionally they take Greeks hunting or attend Athenian drinking-parties; most often they partake in battles, many of them mythical but some, the most interesting, having every appearance of true-to-life operations. In these, the Scyths are fighting in close co-ordination with the hoplites, shooting from between the men of the front ranks, who crouch down and cover the archers and themselves from return fire, perhaps from javelins. The archers in the Attic pictures always take careful aim and shoot horizontally—a sign that they operated at close quarters and against individual targets, unlike the English longbowmen. The sudden appearance of these Scythian troops can only be connected with the tyrant Pisistratus, with whom we have already connected the arrival of the Thracian *pelta* in Greece, also in the hands of mercenaries (p. 79). But this episode was short-lived—perhaps by 500 and certainly by the time of the battle of Marathon, these Scythian archers had disappeared—and further it was, as far as we know, confined to Athens. Perhaps the invasion of their homeland by the Persians under Darius I explains the withdrawal of the Scyths. Polycrates, tyrant of Samos, also used a corps of a thousand bowmen as an instrument for power, and may have recruited them a few years earlier than Pisistratus did his. From the slightly ambiguous word used by Herodotus (III, 45, 4) it seems best to conclude that these were native Samians. *Pl. 38*

For the sling and its users, the evidence from Greece is scarce indeed. By Classical times, the Rhodians had come to excel among the Greeks in the specialized use of the sling, and like the Cretan archers they were often engaged as mercenaries. The sling itself was made or reinforced with dried gut or sinew, a material also used for bow-strings. Ordinary stones could be used as projectiles, like the smooth pebble with which, according to the Bible, David slew Goliath, but far more potent were the specially cast elliptical bullets of lead; their range, according to Xenophon, could be twice that of stones (*Anabasis* III, 3, 16). These seem to become common only in the Classical period, when they are sometimes inscribed. The earliest post-Mycenaean monuments which show the sling in use in a battle belong to the late seventh and early sixth centuries, but they are extremely rare.[54]

Missile-troops of all kinds had to carry a short sword or dagger, in case of being caught with their weapon unserviceable or their projectiles exhausted. For them, as for the hoplites to whom it was also a secondary weapon, size was no longer an advantage in a sword; the result is that it declines both in size and in importance during the seventh and sixth centuries. The commonest type is now a short, crude weapon, with a thick hilt to which a conical pommel was sometimes fixed, and a very broad projecting hand-guard, square-cut on the upper (hilt) side and curving sharply in to the blade on the lower. The blade swells to a maximum width near the tip, making a stout and effective enough weapon for in-fighting.[55] It was carried, by the hoplite at least, in a sheath worn high up under the left arm on a short strap or baldric, enabling it to be quickly drawn with the unencumbered right hand. Only in the late sixth century, a period of military advance in several ways, do we find any revival in the status of the sword. Of other weapons carried by the light-armed, we have only glimpses. The Scythians in their homeland carried a battle-axe, with its main blade running across the axis of the shaft like a modern ice-axe: this is probably what Herodotus calls a *sagaris*, and it is sometimes shown by the Attic vase-painters. Historically it is certainly true that light-armed troops, overshadowed by the prowess of the hoplite, were given an unduly subordinate rôle in the seventh, sixth and even most of the fifth centuries. This situation is reflected artistically, in the lack of accurate portrayals of them in action. *Pls. 51, 52*

The same is true, in an even more marked degree, of early Greek cavalry. In the battle-scenes of the artists and the written accounts (such as they are) of historians, we almost never find cavalry effectively used; this although it had probably played a real part in Dark Age warfare, and although traces of this prowess were preserved in the names, given either to the aristocracy as a whole, or to particular groups, in many cities: the *Hippeis* or knights of Athens, Sparta and Eretria, and the *Hippobotai* of Chalcis are examples. The real function of these 'horsemen' in the age of the hoplite has been thoroughly examined in the case of Athens, the only adequately documented instance for the early period. The most reasonable conclusion is that they used their horses only for transport to the battlefield. They might be attended by a mounted squire, but they were armed as hoplites and, for the actual battle, dismounted and fought in the phalanx. Thus, too, even as late as 418, we find the so-called Hippeis of Sparta fighting as hoplites in the ranks at the battle of Mantinea. The reasons for these limitations to the value of cavalry are clear: two important inventions, those of the stirrup and the horsehoe, had not yet occurred, and Greek war-horses can neither have had reasonable endurance on the rough Greek terrain, nor provided a really safe fighting-platform for mounted soldiers. Often they were ungelded, and breeding was not closely controlled; there are signs of the introduction of fresh foreign blood into the Greek breeds in or around the seventh century.[56]

But this picture was not valid for the whole of Greece. There were states which prided themselves on the prowess of their cavalry, but since they were not productive of early representational art, we have only the few mentions of their cavalry-forces in literature. Thessaly, which possessed the only considerable plain in Greece, was famous from a quite early date for the breeding of horses. Her cavalry was in demand at different times among allies farther south. In the Lelantine War of the late eighth century, when a local dispute between two Euboean cities grew into the first widespread conflict in Greek history, Chalcis called in Thessalian cavalry and with their aid won at least one victory over Eretria. Later, in the First Sacred War fought for the control of Delphi in the opening years of the sixth century, the Thessalians at first bore the brunt of the fighting against the city of Cirrha, which was abusing her control of the sanctuary. Later still we hear of Thessalian help to Athens: on one well-known occasion, against a Spartan invasion in about 510, the Thessalian cavalry turned the scale in favour of the Athenian tyrants, but significantly only after the plain of Phaleron had been cleared and made suitable for a cavalry charge. The Spartans soon afterwards sent a fresh force by a different route; the engagement was on unprepared ground, the verdict was reversed, and the horsemen bolted for Thessaly. In 480, even Thessalian steeds proved far inferior to those of the Persians in point of speed.[57] Boeotian cavalry had also earned a considerable reputation by the fifth century, and in the Persian Wars both Thessaly and Boeotia brought their cavalry in on the Persian side, with differing degrees of justification but to the considerable discomfiture of their fellow-Greeks. It is hard to find archaeological reflection of cavalry prowess, and certainly little or none has yet occurred in these areas. Greek horses were not strong enough to carry the heavy armour of a true charger; bits and other pieces of harness imply little as to the purpose which the horses served. But it is worth pointing out that the simple jointed bit of Mycenaean and Dark Age Greece is replaced in Archaic times by a form with long, curved cheek-pieces, very close to that used by the Assyrians, a notable equestrian people. This form is seen on Corinthian vases from the mid-seventh century onwards. Later the Corinthians were sometimes credited with having invented the bit, and the explanation could be that they were responsible for borrowing this type from its source. A further link with the East is given by the bronze blinkers found on several Greek sites, which are closely associated by both their form and by their decoration with Syrian, Phoenician and Assyrian models,[58] but it is unlikely that their use was for war-horses. The same can be said of the small forehead-guards, also decorated in relief, found at Miletus and Samos. *Pl. 41*

Genuine pieces of horse-armour are very rare on Greek sites, and their distribution is concentrated on the most important remaining cavalry region of the Greek world, Sicily and southern Italy. Here the tactical organization of cavalry had evidently progressed to a degree unmatched in the Greek homeland before the time of Alexander. Gelon of Syracuse in 480 had—presumably to spare, since he offered to send them to the Greek home-land—a force of 2000 cavalry and 2000 light horse; this was not exceptional for Sicily, and it is cavalry which is most prominent in the paltry surviving accounts of Gelon's great victory won later in that year at Himera. The occasional large chamfreins or face-guards, up to eighteen inches in length, which have been found are almost all connected with western Greece, either from having been found there, or by their artistic style; one or two have appeared at Olympia.[59]

It remains only to say a word about the chariot. It is likely that some of the harness found on eastern Greek sites belonged to driven horses, and the Lydians and other neighbouring peoples were possibly still using chariots in the Archaic period. From Boeotia there is an Archaic terracotta model chariot, with a hoplite mounted beside a lightly-armed driver; certainly anachronistic as far as real-life warfare is concerned, this monument is presumably meant to portray heroic practice. We have no evidence for thinking that these or any other Greeks in the Aegean area were still using the war-chariot. It was different in Cyprus, where we still read of chariots in a battle at the beginning of the fifth century, and where some archaeological reflection can be seen in a peculiar type of horse's face-armour found, and perhaps in the occurrence of burials with a funerary cart or chariot. Cyrene and Barca, where the North African plains provided suitable ground and the chariot-using Egyptians and Libyans a model, were among the few other Greek communities which practised chariot-warfare; we still find this arm being taken seriously there in the fourth century. One last oddity of Greek warfare, to all appearances an Ionian speciality, was the use of war-dogs in battle.[60] *Pl. 36*

45   Attic red-figure kylix of the early fifth century showing young men putting on their armour. The painting shows how the composite corslet was worn; first it was fastened over the chest (central figure), then the flaps were drawn down over the shoulders (right-hand figure) and attached by laces to the body of the corslet. Argive shields, still of the traditional style, and Corinthian helmets are awaiting their owners, and a bronze greave is being slipped on. See pp. 90-1, 53.

46 Red-figure amphora, dating from after the Persian Wars, showing a Greek
hoplite attacking a Persian soldier. The barbarian is, to all appearances, protected
from head to foot, but only by quilted or leather garments; the long spear and heavy
shield of the Greek proved their superiority in many engagements. See pp. 100–1.

47-49 Excavations at Paphos in Cyprus in 1950-55 revealed a large ditch and mound roughly corresponding in date to the Persian siege-operations in the island (498 BC) reported by Herodotus. The Corinthian helmet (*above, left*) is a relic of the fighting recovered from the mound (see p. 66). *Below, right:* An example of a later form of Corinthian helmet (see pp. 93-4) *Above, right:* An exceptionally well-preserved Chalcidian helmet, from near Salonika, now in the British Museum. See p. 116.

50-52 *Left:* Short one-edged slashing sword of a type often used for an over-hand stroke. See p. 97. *Right and centre:* Broad-bladed short sword and scabbard. Both these sword types were used by the hoplites for close fighting if the spear should be lost or broken, as well as by other troops. Lengths about 55 cm. See pp. 84-5.

CHAPTER IV

THE GREAT WARS

THE GREAT CONFLICTS of the fifth century usually form the centre-piece of Greek history, and this may seem a belated stage at which to be approaching them. But the fact is that, in the field of armament, the pioneer and experimental achievements had almost all taken place before this time. The forging of the main military instrument, the hoplite, was virtually complete; only a few timely modifications were incorporated in the generation before the onset of the Persians. The light-armed troops and cavalry did not, partly because they were not allowed to, play a major part in the Persian Wars, against an enemy who was distinctly better equipped in both these arms. By the time of the Pelo-ponnesian War fifty years later, many Greeks were realizing that their grandfathers had triumphed in spite of, not because of, this neglect, and were beginning to exploit some of the possibilities of lighter-armed infantry at least. But from all that we know of the armament and tactics of the land-battles against the Persians, they could have been fought along very similar lines at any time in the previous century and a half, as far as the Greeks were con-cerned. There is another factor which makes for imbalance in the study of Greek arms, and this is the progressive deterioration of our evidence. The first and most serious blow falls when the Greeks generally discontinue the practice of burial with weapons. Dedi-cations in the sanctuaries are the best source of evidence for some two centuries thereafter, but for various reasons—one of them no doubt the sheer congestion which had arisen—the quantity of these falls off at many sites in the Classical period, as compared with the Archaic. Meanwhile the most important class of repre-sentational evidence, the vase-paintings, declines sharply in

geographical extent and, somewhat later, in quality, before
ceasing altogether. The increase in written evidence might com-
pensate for all this, but scarcely does so; for one thing, the hoplite and his arms were no longer either a novelty or a rarity, and
the descriptive passages of a Tyrtaeus or Alcaeus, riddled with
ambiguities though they may be, find no place in the more
sophisticated literature of the fifth century. Nonetheless, we have
in this period, for the first time, contemporary or near-contemporary prose accounts of warfare, and that is much.

The hoplite, recognized if not fully accepted throughout the
Greek world, had developed so little by the mid-sixth century
that some changes may well have been thought overdue. The
most general feeling seems to have been that his body-armour
was too heavy and unwieldy. One time-honoured alternative
which avoided this fault was the corslet of linen. This was old
enough to appear in the *Iliad*, where Ajax the lesser and Amphion
are both 'linen-corseleted' (II, 529, 830); and indeed it may have
been used by the Mycenaeans of the Shaft-grave period, as we
have seen (p. 18). Linen in multiple layers, quilted together, has
a long history as a defensive material and should not be under-
rated. At the beginning of the sixth century, the corslets mentioned by Alcaeus in his list of armour (p. 64) are of linen; later
in the century the Egyptian Pharaoh Amasis dedicated an elaborate
and famous example at Lindos and sent another to Sparta; in
the Persian Wars we find it worn by the Assyrian troops of
Xerxes.[1] But it was only in the second half of this century that
the Greeks devised a compromise that would combine the
flexibility and ventilation of the linen corslet with the impene-
trability of the all-bronze cuirass. We see the new corslet on
many of the finer monuments of the later Archaic period, but
perhaps its clearest portrayal is on the memorable figure of
Achilles on a red-figure vase of about 450. It was a composite
affair, fastening down the front. Two large shoulder-pieces
(*epōmides*) were permanently attached at the back, brought
over the shoulders, and fastened by laces to the chest. They were
broad for most of their length, but had narrower extensions at
the front; in general they form the most conspicuous part of the

corslet.[2] The body of the garment extended well below the
waist, with a sort of skirt formed of one or two rows of leather
flaps (*pteruges*). It is not easy to tell how far it was metallic, and a
considerable variety in materials was evidently possible for the
main part of the corslet, from the neck-line to the waist. One
variant of the corslet had this zone partly covered in metal
scales, either small and shaped like a fish's, or larger and oblong.
This is the first important use in Greece of a long-lived and
widely favoured form of protection. It was worn by many Near
Eastern peoples, including the Persians (p. 101), and its home
according to Herodotus was Egypt; it was adopted in two areas
on the edge of the Greek world, Cyprus and the Crimea. But in
Greece proper, actual fragments are seldom found, and we
cannot tell whether they belonged to all-scale corslets on the
Oriental model, or to partly-scaled ones of the new Greek type.
In the latter case, to judge from the pictures, scales when they
occurred were often confined to the sides, leaving a plain vertical
band in front. But nearly as often the artists show the whole
corslet as a surface of plain flexible material, probably leather and
certainly non-metallic, to which bands or plates of bronze are
apparently attached. Of this type of corslet in general, almost the
only other traces to be recovered in modern times have been
the decorative bronze finials fixed to the front extensions of the
shoulder-pieces.[3] *Pls. 39, 42, 45*

Arming-scenes on vases, showing this type of corslet, are very
common about the time of the Persian Wars, and this was no
doubt the predominant form worn by the hoplites on the Greek
side. A cast of the grave-stele of Aristion, who wears this type
of armour, has now been erected on the battlefield of Marathon,
a fitting monument although its date is somewhat earlier than
that of the battle. The historical significance of this change in
armour was quite far-reaching. In art, we see a marked increase
in the number of pictures of running hoplites, in contrast to the
rather static battles of earlier Archaic art; while at Marathon
the Athenian hoplites, coming within range of the Persian archers
and unprotected by any archers of their own, dismayed the enemy
by charging them at a run. Such exertion was probably intolerably

uncomfortable and exhausting in the old 'bell' corslet, but now it had evidently become possible. It may be no coincidence that the race in armour at the Olympic games was instituted at this time, in the sixty-fifth Olympiad (520 BC).[4]

But although the 'bell' corslet was now rendered obsolete throughout Greece, the type we have been describing was not its only successor. In the early part of the fifth century we can follow the tentative development of another type, closer to the 'bell' corslet in that it, too, consisted basically of two bronze plates, front and rear, joining down the sides. But in place of the uncompromising shape and jutting rim of the old type, it is carefully shaped to fit the human torso, and reproduces as its decoration the main muscles of the chest and abdomen, somewhat in the manner of contemporary (or earlier) sculpture. In front, the lower rim curves downwards to protect the stomach and up again to the hips; below are usually attached *pteruges*, sometimes of palm-leaf shape, sometimes of the special box-pleat form of the other Classical type of corslet (p. 91). Being predominantly metal, several examples of this type have survived, although almost all come either from Etruscan tombs or from sites in southern Italy.[5] They mostly belong to the fourth century or later, and testify to the long life and wide extent of this form. It is presumably corslets of this type which are made by the armourer Pistias, whom Socrates visits in an anecdote of Xenophon's (*Memorabilia* III, 10, 9); great stress is laid there on the need for a good fit, and on the high price which customers are prepared to pay for it. In Aristophanes' *Peace* (line 1224) a coarser use is suggested for a plate-corslet of this type.

Of the other armour of the Archaic hoplite, the greave had proved adequate and needed little modification. By the later sixth century it had been shaped to fit the leg as closely as possible; fifth-century examples are distinguishable, if at all, by their decoration. But we should mention here a number of supplementary pieces of armour which the richer hoplite occasionally adopted, mostly during the sixth century. Perhaps the commonest of these, to judge from the number of actual examples found, were the bronze ankle-guards; they are frequent at Olympia, and there are again some later examples from southern Italy. They are somewhat in the shape of modern spats, but moulded to fit the ankle-bone; in art they can seldom be seen. Next come the protective pieces for the upper and lower arm, the rerebrace and vambrace of medieval chivalry. The former was far the commoner: it is worn by Achilles in Exekias' famous vase-painting of the dice-game with Ajax at Troy, and some fine examples have occurred at Olympia, decorated on the analogy of greaves in imitation of the shape of the upper-arm muscles. They were normally worn on the right arm only, the left being pro-tected by the shield. Forearm-guards are less often depicted and hardly ever found. It is noteworthy that both are shown in Etruscan art; Etruria was particularly enthusiastic in emulating the advances made in Greek armament, and often did so when they were falling out of favour in Greece itself. The thigh-guard (*parameridion*) is comparatively frequent in sixth-century art, but almost absent from Greece thereafter; actual finds are curiously few.[6] These objects were never anything more than optional accessories for the really well-equipped hoplite, and were per-haps partly for ceremonial use. Even though the vase-paintings are exaggerated in the degree of nudity they often show, it is clear that the ordinary Greek hoplite never attempted to acquire the *cap-à-pie* protection of the medieval knight, and that by the fifth century he had come to give first priority to mobility. *Pl. 37*

The wide range of helmets devised in the seventh and sixth centuries also sufficed for the needs of the Persian Wars. Two types in turn predominate, the almost indestructible Corinthian and the newer Attic. The Corinthian helmet, developing con-tinuously, had reached a very advanced form by the late sixth century. Many of the dedicated examples have their cheek-pieces bent back, a practice akin to the ritual 'killing' of weapons, noted earlier (p. 37). The earlier improved models, with their decorated rims and longer and lower shape, had notches or recesses in the sides to enable the helmet to settle squarely on the neck and shoulders. A new standard form then grew out of these, in which the once vertical edges of the cheek-piece and nose-guard now jutted forwards at a raking angle, the nose-guard being in a rather graceful tongue-shape, while the whole skull-piece was set off from the rest of the helmet by a prominent plastic ridge, running from above the forehead diagonally down to the nape of the neck. Below this, the neck-guard was recessed inwards and then jutted out at the rim. There is sometimes an aperture for the ear as in the Chalcidian type (p. 70). When not in action, the hoplite could push such a helmet upwards and rest it on the back of his head. The Corinthian helmet seems to have been widely worn down to the early fifth century; but after this it appears to go rather abruptly out of use, surviving only in a few artistic conventions, as on portrait-heads of generals, and in a debased form in southern Italy.[7] In Athens and perhaps other cities, the Attic helmet was already in vogue before this happened; one may observe the strikingly small version, little more than a cap, worn by the hoplite Aristion. This may indeed be a distinct and even lighter head-piece, the *pilos* which Thucydides says the Spartan hoplites were wearing in 425 (IV, 34, 3). Clearly, in the helmet as in body-armour, the main tendency from the late sixth century onwards is towards lightness. *Pl. 48*

Here we may deal with a question posed by a remark of Demosthenes (LIX, 94): he says that, in a painting by Mikon of the battle of Marathon, the Plataean hoplites are distinguished (primarily from the Athenians) by the Boeotian helmets which they wear. Mikon was probably a boy at the time of the battle and worked on the mural perhaps thirty years later, so that he is unlikely to have committed an anachronism. Which, among the helmet-types of the early fifth century, is the 'Boeotian'? Our best clue is given by Xenophon (*On Horsemanship* XII, 3) who recommends it for cavalry because it gives good visibility; it must therefore be one of the open-faced types, but not the Attic which the Athenians wore. There is a form for which a local connection with Boeotia is established by grave-reliefs; like the *pilos*, it is little more than a metallic hat, with downward-sloping brim. What is perhaps an early stage in the development of this type can be seen on vases of Mikon's period, including one of the Amazon battle-scenes which has actually been connected with Mikon's work; this seems, therefore, the happiest identification for the Boeotian helmet. It bears a marked resemblance to the ordinary hat or *petasos* of the Greeks, much favoured by the god Hermes.[8] *Pl. 58*

To this same period, soon after the Persian Wars, belongs another and more conspicuous innovation in Greek helmet-types. Again the new helmet seems to be based on an everyday hat, but this time its model is a form of cap worn in Thrace, and by Thracians in Greek art. The cap is made of animal-skin or other soft material, sometimes rising to a point at the top but more often to a forward-pointing peak, like the better-known 'Phrygian bonnet'. It also has some kind of reinforced band or hem running across the forehead. The helmet repeats this shape, often to the point of simulating the peak in bronze. Its most prominent feature is the combined forehead-guard and eye-shade, which juts slightly forward but is reminiscent of the corresponding feature on the cap. With the example of the mis-named 'Illyrian' helmet before us we should be cautious in apply-ing regional names, but in this case it seems fair to call the helmet Thracian. The 'Illyrian' helmet, incidentally, now long since made in one piece, is still present in art and in actual finds of the fifth century in Greece proper, in addition to its great popularity farther north.[9] *Pl. 53*

Throughout the fifth century, shield-forms remained more or less constant: for the light-armed, the *pelta* of crescent or round shape, whose wicker-work base is sometimes shown in the paintings; and for the hoplite the great round shield, by now definitely called Argive. It is in red-figure scenes that we see most clearly how the handles of the hoplite shield were now arranged: the *porpax* or arm-band remained much the same, but by this time the *antilabē* was formed by running a cord all round the shield on a series of about half a dozen studs, some little way in from the rim, to which decorative tassels were often attached. Many of these bronze studs have been found loose in the excava-tions at Olympia. By this arrangement, the hoplite gripped the section of the cord which lay at the position of his left hand, but he had plenty of spare cord if it should break. The aspect to which perhaps the greatest study has been given is that of the devices on

the hoplite shield in sixth- and fifth-century art.[10] We have seen
(p. 67) that certain cities used a distinctive blazon for their hoplites' shields, often the initial letter of the city's name. But attempts
have been made to recognize, in the pictorial blazons shown on
Attic vases, the badges of individual families in Athens. Most
convincing perhaps was the theory that the *triskeles* represented
the Alcmaeonids and their dependants, since in this case there
was some literary evidence, albeit ambiguous, from Aristophanes
(*Lysistrata* 664). But even this identification is open to serious
criticism, and the others are far weaker. Since shield-devices in
Greek art tend to repeat themselves in widely-separated periods
and regions, it seems wisest to attach no significance to them but a
purely artistic one. Individual vase-painters, for instance, have
been shown to favour certain devices. Olympia has yielded plenty
of actual blazons; they are thin sheets of beaten bronze, cut to the
requisite shape and often further decorated by incision. The most
popular devices are birds and animals, but it is worth noting that
in both finds and representations the shape of the long-obsolete
'Boeotian' shield is used as a blazon for a real hoplite shield.[11]

In weapons of attack a few additions were made in the Classical
period. Spearheads, spear-butts and javelin-heads show perhaps
the least alteration, for their purpose and use remained unchanged.
The spear-butt as we saw is often of bronze, and several inscribed
examples of fifth century date survive. But a more surprising
fact, that has emerged from excavations at Olympia and other
sanctuary-sites, is that spearheads too, after having for centuries
been made almost exclusively of iron, show a resurgence of
bronze in the sixth and perhaps the fifth centuries. To suggest
that a shortage of iron, or any other economic factor, lay behind
this would be mere guesswork; at least as important a reason
may have been the desire for decorative effect, to which bronze
lent itself better than iron. Some of the most spectacular, if
least useful, dedications at Olympia and elsewhere are huge
spearheads, well over three feet long with broad blades decorated
in incision, which are quite un-Greek in conception and undoubtedly come from Sicily or southern Italy. They resemble
native Italian shapes, but on this scale their use must have been

purely ceremonial. In general, the dedications at sanctuaries would naturally be of finer quality than the average, and we may safely assume that the ordinary Greek hoplite or peltast still used a spear tipped with the plainer but deadlier iron. The extraordinarily persistent theme in the vase-paintings, of a hoplite armed with *two* spears, is still alive in the late sixth century and does not finally die out until the fifth. We have confirmation, from a remark in a dialogue of Plato and a line of Euripides, that a single spear had become the standard equipment by the late fifth century.[12]

A more significant change had come about with the introduction to Greece of a new type of sword. The 'Griffzungenschwert' was now perhaps extinct here, while the dominant weapon of the sixth century, the stout slashing-sword with cruciform hand-guard and swelling blade (pp. 84–5), remained in use. But it was eclipsed by the appearance of a more specialized cutting-weapon: a single-edged, slightly curved short sword, very like the Gurkha kukri, which was regularly used in a downward slash, brought from far behind the left shoulder in an overhead motion. Both the cutting edge and the back were convex, weighting the weapon heavily towards the tip; the hilt had a hand-guard and pommel which projected on the cutting side only, and was frequently shaped like a sitting bird with the head serving as a pommel. This sword would certainly be covered by the old and widely-applied Greek term *machaira*, and it may also have borne the stricter name of *kopis*; the Greeks seem to have been highly inconsistent in their nomenclature of weapons. There are earlier precedents for this shape in Greece, among both weapons and cleavers or other domestic instruments; but the sudden onset of the new sword in Greek battle-scenes of the latest sixth and fifth centuries suggests either a marked advance in design or a borrowing from abroad. It may well have had an ancestry among the curved weapons associated with the Persians and other Orientals by the Greeks; if it is the *kopis*, it almost certainly did. It may even have acquired a prestige value from the fact that, according to the almost unanimous testimony of Athenian artists, Harmodius struck down the tyrant Hipparchus in 514 BC with a sword of this type, and with its characteristic overhand stroke.[13] Thereafter it becomes so common that we must believe that hoplites really used it; they remained primarily spearmen as ever, but when their spears broke they would fall back on this weapon for hand-to-hand fighting, as we read that the 300 Spartans did in the later stages of the battle of Thermopylae (Herodotus VII, 224). *Pls. 44, 50–2*

Some attention to light-armed troops was long overdue in Greek warfare, and we can at last detect the growth of organized peltast-forces, though scarcely before the Peloponnesian War. Cleon took a force from Aenos in Thrace with him to Sphacteria in 425, to good effect. Ironically, it was by the hand of a Thracian peltast that he himself was to meet death three years later when, on the initiative of Brasidas, Sparta had learned and applied the same lesson (Thucydides IV, 28; V, 6 and 10). In Boeotia, we hear of a special corps of highly mobile infantry called the *hamippoi* (V, 57; *cf.* Xenophon, *Hellenica* VII, 5, 23). But even here, it is the allies of the two great powers who are showing the way, not those powers themselves; the next stage had to wait until later still (p. 110). Equally important, and traceable rather earlier, is the increase in attention paid to archery in the fifth century; here Athens seems to keep up with other states. The best pointer to the change is perhaps given by the marked contrast between the Persian Wars and the Peloponnesian War towards the end of the century. At Marathon we hear that the Athenians were without archers, their Scythian experiment (pp. 83–4) being apparently terminated. But very soon afterwards the gap was filled—according to Ctesias, by the hiring of Cretans. The new force of archers proved its worth against the Persians under Xerxes, particularly at Salamis. Perhaps because of this, archery achieved a progressively higher status at Athens in the ensuing years. Before the middle of the century, Athenian citizens were trained as archers, and *toxarchoi* or Captains of Bowmen appointed. By the beginning of the Peloponnesian War Athens even had mounted bowmen, the last word (and a decidedly un-Greek one) in specialized warfare. The prestige of the bow may have been boosted by the action on Sphacteria in 425, when a force of

Spartan hoplites was worn down until, unprecedentedly, it surrendered; in the following year, we find the Spartans taking the unusual step of organizing a corps of cavalry and archers. Archers, with slingers and javelin-throwers, were included in substantial numbers in the great Athenian expedition to Sicily in 415. Here they were faced by an enemy who, characteristically, had left mainland Greece far behind in the development of this arm: even in 480, Gelon of Syracuse had commanded a force of 2000 archers.[14]

We can trace some of the stages in this development in the archaeological record. Evidence for the bow, from scenes which can purport to represent real-life battles, is now virtually non-existent. We have only the repeated portrayal of Heracles (normally with the Scythian bow), and Apollo and Artemis (normally with the 'self' bow, sometimes with the single-curved composite type with reflexed tips); Amazons, too, are frequently given the Scythian bow. But finds of arrowheads are more helpful. They are, in many periods of antiquity, the only evidence still recoverable from the sites of battles and sieges, having escaped the scrap-hunters. In London and in Karlsruhe there are collections of arrow-heads, with a few other weapons, including sling-bullets, which purport to be from the field of Marathon. We cannot really trust such provenances, which are frequently invented by the vendors of antiquities to increase the interest of their wares. Many of the heads are of the small Scythian bronze type; since it is evident that any genuine arrowheads from Marathon must have been fired by the Persian army, one may infer that the new enemies of Greece, like the Lydians before them, had adopted this serviceable type of arrow. In any case they had done so by 480, for excavations in the pass of Thermopylae, where once again the Persians alone had archers, revealed a mass of arrowheads exclusively of this class. Later in the same year occurred an event less celebrated in Greek annals, the temporary abandonment of the city of Athens to the Persians. The Acropolis was held for a time (Herodotus VIII, 51-3), and only after a barrage of arrows was fired from the Areopagus and elsewhere did the Persians obtain success. Here too, on the Acropolis slopes, the excavators found Scythian arrowheads heavily preponderant.[15]

Only rarely can other weapons or pieces of armour be used to illustrate known historical events in the way that arrowheads can; and conversely, the rays of light that they have occasionally shed have most often fallen in places otherwise quite dark. Thus, the most substantial dedication of arms recovered from the finds at Olympia consists of two Corinthian helmets and seven or eight hoplite shields, all inscribed with the formula 'The Argives dedicated, from the Corinthians'. From the style of script and armour, a victory must have been won by Argos over Corinth in the period round 500 BC or a little later, but it is a victory otherwise lost to posterity. To the same or a slightly later period belong other unrecorded victories—by Zankle over Rhegion, by a league of three other southern Italian colonies over Kroton, and in the second half of the fifth century by Tarentum over Thurii; those on the Greek mainland include, surprisingly, a fifth-century victory by the men of Methana over the Spartans. Just occasionally, dedications of arms have been associated with less obscure events. Thus at Olympia was found a Corinthian helmet of up-to-date, rakish cut, though in very poor condition, dedicated by no less a person than Miltiades, the victor of Marathon; but the inscription gives no further indication of the circumstances. A more recent discovery at Olympia was a bronze helmet of very simple form, inscribed 'The Athenians to Zeus, having got it from the Medes'. It undoubtedly dates from the early fifth century, but there is no way of telling whether it was booty from Marathon (as at first glance the dedication by 'the Athenians' alone might suggest) or one of the later battles. Probably it was worn by a cavalryman (*cf.* Herodotus VII, 84); it is an interesting side-light on the Greek lack of sentimentality that this trophy was already thrown down and buried by 450. Again, the British Museum possesses perhaps the best-known of all dedications of armour, the Etruscan pot-shaped helmet captured by Hieron of Syracuse in his victory at the naval battle of Cumae in 474; it was dedicated at Olympia (always favoured by the western Greeks), found in the early nineteenth century and presented to King George IV. Another Syracusan dedication—a shield captured from the Acragantines —may belong to a victory won in 445 (Diodorus XII, 8).[16] But in the main, the most valuable lesson to be drawn from such archaeological finds as these, themselves only a tiny proportion of what was originally dedicated, is the fragmentary nature of our written sources for the political history of sixth- and fifth-century Greece.

The rather rudimentary shape of the barbarian helmets—the Persian one is of a type which had been in use for three centuries or more in the Near East—brings us to another, and perhaps the most important, aspect of Greek armour and arms: their superiority to those of other nations at the time. The differences between Greek and Persian armament were clear, and were remembered in some detail by those vase-painters who in subsequent years commemorated the Persian Wars in battle-scenes. But by later in the century, men like the sculptor of the 'Plataea' frieze on the temple of Nike at Athens unhesitatingly put aesthetic aims before historical realism.[17] Herodotus lists the equipment of the Persian infantryman in 480 (VII, 61): on the head, a loose cloth covering, the *tiara*; on the body, the sleeved iron scale-corslet (vase-painters sometimes show a sleeveless jerkin worn over this); trousers on the legs; the wicker *gerrhon* (p. 78) for a shield; short spear, large bow and cane arrows, and dagger. Defensively in the helmet, shield and greaves and offensively in the length of spear, it would seem that the Greeks had a clear advantage in hand-to-hand infantry battle; this superiority is confirmed by a number of Greek writers, and must reflect contemporary Greek opinion as well. It is a theme of Herodotus' which extends back to before the Persian invasions: Aristagoras of Miletus, visiting Sparta to ask for support in the rising of the Ionian Greeks against the Persians, tells the Spartan king that the barbarians are by no means formidable enemies, fighting as they do with bows and short spears (V, 49, 5). The theme of the smallness of Persian arms is taken up again in the account of Thermopylae (VII, 211, 2) where this puts the Persians at a disadvantage in close combat with the Spartan hoplites. The smaller and lighter

Persian shields must also have been ill-suited for this sort of fighting, as was indeed observed by the source of the account of this battle given in the much later historian Diodorus (XI, 7). At Plataea in the following year (479), Herodotus makes the more general point that the Persians were weakened by their lack of armour; they are *anhoploi* against *hoplitai*, and can hardly hope to win in such a contest (IX, 62, 4 and 63, 3); there is no mention in this context of the scale-corslet of the Persians, even though the troops concerned were a picked Persian élite of a thousand. In later writers the same assumption recurs, as in Pausanias' story of a small Megarian force ambushing a much larger Persian column (I, 40, 2). There is no reason to doubt this unanimous verdict of the Greek historians, which would reduce rather than enhance the glory of their country's victories. But a deeper lesson was open to those who had eyes to see: namely that, had the Persians been able to give battle more often by other means than the heavy infantry mêlée, or even simply to defer action for longer, the result of the war might have been very different. *Pl. 46*

This book is not primarily concerned with tactics, but it is worth pausing for a moment to look more closely at these feats of the Greek hoplite—Marathon, Thermopylae, Plataea. Each took place in a profoundly different situation, and shows the advantages and weaknesses of the hoplite method in a different light. Marathon, the first ancient battle which offers a field for true criticism, was also the first critical test for the hoplite. Each side already had a fair basis for an estimate of the other's potentialities, and in a purely tactical sense the overriding aim of the Greeks must have been to get to close quarters before the Persian archers and cavalry could take their toll. The fact that the Persian cavalry played no effective part in the battle is not grounds for the repeated modern assertion that they had been re-embarked before it began; more probably, they were as nonplussed as the rest of their army by the speedy advance which the Athenian hoplites with their new mobility (p. 91) achieved. The hoplite's powers of resistance to missile-fire and cavalry alike were considerable, and may or may not have been specifically put to the test at Marathon. What was now beyond argument was that (as the Greeks had hoped) the Persians had nothing that could stand up to the hoplite fighting in deep phalanx formation, as on the Athenian wings. Thermopylae, the only one of these battles which did not end in their victory, was nevertheless in some ways the most striking vindication of all for the hoplites. Whatever the strategic rights and wrongs of Leonidas' stand, his choice of ground was faultless, not merely for a battle in general but for a hoplite battle: a passage that was not only narrow, but flat. The pass was about fifty feet wide at Thermopylae itself (Herodotus VII, 176, 2), and a phalanx of 300 could hold this frontage in about twice the depth normal for this period; though in the event, the Spartan tactics were clearly more mobile and unorthodox, at least on the first day (VII, 211), than those of the ordinary phalanx. The outflanking movement which finally destroyed the Spartans was a breach of the code, half-religious if not almost sporting, which seems to have governed the attitude to hoplite warfare in Classical times. Only rarely do the Greeks show such an eye for the strategic main chance—Myronides surprising the Corinthians while they were setting up a trophy is one example (Thucydides I, 105)—until much later, when the set-piece hoplite battle had become largely a thing of the past. At Plataea, finally, Pausanias' larger and more motley Greek army had to face a greater threat from cavalry and archers, and a much less advantageous natural situation, than either Miltiades at Marathon or Leonidas at Thermopylae. But once again, the Persian cavalry failed to force a decision and again, after much inconsequential manoeuvring, the conclusive phase of the battle was provoked by a hoplite charge (IX, 62). It was only natural that, in the aftermath of these battles, the Greeks dwelt more on the proven fact of their hoplites' quality, than on the many unattractive might-have-beens.

But there are already signs, in the period just after the Persian Wars, that there were Greek soldiers on whom the lesson had not been wholly lost, and who accordingly took steps to repair their cities' deficiencies in the other military branches, such as light missile-throwing troops and cavalry. The growing prowess of the bow and other missile-weapons is probably reflected in the protective apron, apparently of leather, often attached in the period after the Persian Wars to the lower rim of the hoplite shield. This probably supplemented the greaves in their function as a barrier against missiles (Alcaeus' phrase, p. 64)—a function which will also explain why, in the more backward parts of Greece as in barbarian Europe, the greave is found more commonly and earlier than any other part of the panoply. Archers, as we have seen, appear with increasing frequency in the historical records. But an equally telling indication is the attention now paid to cavalry. In Athens, where the force of mounted hoplites had for long been 'cavalry' only in name (p. 85), there was now a change of attitude. Well before the Peloponnesian War broke out in 431, a true cavalry force had been raised, and it soon reached a strength of 1000, a figure retained for a century or more. This force was a 'light brigade', armed with an eye to its functions and the limitations of its mounts. Some of these cavalrymen carried two light javelins, others a single thrusting-spear lighter than the hoplite's. Armour later became progressively regarded as more important for cavalry, but it was at first usually light and non-metallic, as we learn from Xenophon's treatise (p. 109 below), leather boots for example, being preferred to greaves. The broad-brimmed hat or *petasos* was evidently worn at least as much as a helmet. No shield was carried by the cavalry when mounted. Now, or perhaps rather later, a much harsher bit was beginning to be introduced to Greece, with spiked rollers for the sides of the horse's mouth.[18]

The Athenian cavalry was recruited from the young men of the richest families, and though it performed some good services in this early period, it carried a social prestige out of all proportion to its military effect. Even in the Peloponnesian War we find it playing a rather minor rôle, while Sparta was, typically, even further behind in both development and numbers of cavalry. But for the horsemen and light-armed troops of other cities, the first ten years of the war provided a number of shining successes won against hoplites. For example, at Spartolus in 429 a force of 2000 Athenian hoplites, having worsted their Chalcidian opposite numbers, were engaged, harassed and finally routed by the

53 Thracian helmet. This form of helmet developed in the fifth century from a type of leather cap, and is distinguished from earlier types by its pronounced peak and crenellated cheek-pieces. See p. 95.

54 Frieze of warriors from the 'Nereid Monument', a funerary monument from Xanthos in Lycia dated about 400 BC. It shows the close formation of the Greek hoplite phalanx, necessary if each man was to be sheltered by his right-hand neighbour's shield. The gesticulating figure is presumably an officer, serving in the line of battle. See pp. 54, 61-2, 105.

55-56 The inscription on the tomb-stone of Dexileos (*left*) shows that this young Athenian cavalryman was killed at Corinth in 394 BC at the age of twenty. See p. 109. Considerable artistic licence has been employed in showing the adversaries so lightly clothed; and a more realistic representation is the stele of Aristonautes, (*above*), an Athenian soldier of the late fourth century, who wears a 'muscle' cuirass with *pteruges* and carries the full equipment of his day. See pp. 125-6.

57 Terracotta statuette of a war-elephant of Antiochus I of Syria (280-261 BC) over-powering a Galatian foe, who carries the light oval shield called the *thureos*. See p. 123.

Chalcidian cavalry and peltasts, losing 430 dead including all three of their generals (Thucydides II, 79). Three years later another Athenian commander, Demosthenes, could still be persuaded to launch a similar force, in far worse country, against the lightly-armoured Aetolians, in the hope of an easy victory but with scarcely less disastrous results (III, 94 and 97-8); in 425 however he was able to participate in the more famous victory on the island of Sphacteria (p. 98), where even Spartan hoplites had to bow to the archers and javelin-throwers after these had taken them in the rear. At Delium a year later, a pitched and evenly-fought hoplite battle between the Athenians and Boeotians was decided by the appearance of a handful of Boeotian cavalry; these further harassed the retreating Athenians, who had foolishly sent their light-armed troops on ahead, and Athens lost nearly a thousand hoplite dead, again including the general (IV, 96 and 101). At Amphipolis, finally, in 422 Athenian hoplites again found themselves defeated—taken in the flank this time—by a mixed but predominantly peltast and cavalry force under Brasidas (V, 10), an experience which repeated some features of the Spartolus disaster in this same part of Greece. A material relic of the third of these victories, one of the very few that survive from the Peloponnesian War, was excavated in the market-place at Athens: a hoplite shield, inscribed 'The Athenians from the Lacedaemonians, from Pylos', one of a group whose preservation is recorded by Pausanias (I, 15, 4). The form of the shield is unaltered, a monument to Spartan and indeed Greek conservatism in warfare.[19] *Pl. 19*

In the second part of the war, there are signs of a more realistic appraisal of the value of different arms in Athens. The Athenians in 418 took a detachment of cavalry which, as Thucydides realized, saved their hoplites from heavy losses at the battle of Mantinea (V, 73). This battle incidentally provides a good instance of tactical insight on the part of a hoplite commander. Noting the natural tendency of men in the phalanx to edge to the right on joining battle, in order to make sure of the protection of their right-hand neighbour's shield, Agis of Sparta ordered reinforcements to be sent to his own left to save it from being outflanked by the enemy's right wing. The order was given too late and the manœuvre was a failure, Agis gaining victory by other means; but the idea had been sound enough. Three years later, on Nicias' insistence, Athens equipped her Sicilian expedition and its later reinforcements with a good number of missile-troops, including Cretan mercenary archers and a much larger number of Rhodian slingers. Even now, however, they could do little to match the formidable Syracusan cavalry. The original expedition was accompanied by a paltry thirty horses, and when reinforcements were urgently demanded in the following year, cavalrymen were sent with their saddles and bridles but without mounts, which were to be provided on their arrival in Sicily—a policy which speaks poorly indeed for the degree of training expected of horse and rider (Thucydides VI, 43 and 94; cf. VII, 58). Predictably, the Athenian army received its *coup-de-grâce* under a hail of Syracusan javelins and missiles, hemmed in by the enemy cavalry. The closing years of the war saw few land actions, although both light-armed troops and hoplites repeatedly proved their value at sea, in missile fire and boarding-tactics.

Another lesson now learned, somewhat belatedly, by the Athenians and their opponents in mainland Greece was the value of the professional mercenary.[20] It is on the Peloponnesian side that we see them employed at first: hoplite mercenaries from the Peloponnese itself (perhaps Arcadia) were employed by the Corinthians at Potidaea in 432, and later Brasidas had both Peloponnesian and Thracian mercenaries. Arcadians were even in Persian and Colophonian service in 427 (Thucydides I, 60; IV, 80; V, 6; III, 34). The Athenians, perhaps cut off from the richest sources of mercenary hoplites and peltasts, were nevertheless employing Mantineans, as well as Cretan missile-troops, by 415 (see above); in the next year they sent home some Thracian mercenary peltasts who had arrived too late for the Sicilian expedition, on the grounds that their pay (a drachma a day) made them an excessive luxury (VII, 27). Here too mainland Greece was backward by comparison with Sicily: Hippocrates of Gela was already, it seems, employing mercenaries at the very beginning of the century, and his successor Gelon is said to have given the citizenship of Syracuse to no less than 10,000 of them.[20] But by the end of the Peloponnesian War all the many new features —the power of the javelin and arrow, the usefulness of cavalry as a defensive or holding force, the value of the mercenary—had left a permanent mark in the Greek military history. In warfare as in much else, the Peloponnesian War is the end of a chapter.

At this period, incidentally, we have our first indications of a new aspect of armour and weapons: their cost. Weapons were not expensive—an Athenian inscription of 415 gives prices (admittedly second-hand) of 2 drachmai for a javelin and $1\frac{2}{3}$ for a spear without spear-butt; this makes an interesting comparison with the contemporary rate of pay for Athenian hoplites, about a drachma a day plus food-allowance. On the other hand, Aristophanes' *Peace*, a few years earlier has a scene in which armourers of various kinds, put out of business by the signing of an armistice, place extremely high values on their goods: 10 mnai or 1000 drachmai for a corslet, 100 drachmai for a helmet, 60 for a trumpet.[21] It would be misleading to give modern equivalents, but the figures are so high that a degree of comic exaggeration is rightly suspected. The passage at least illustrates the degree of specialization, whereby a different branch of the trade was concerned with each article of armour.

There are obvious changes in the ensuing wars, as described in the pages of Xenophon. He himself partook, only a few years after the Peloponnesian War, in that most significant episode, the march of the Ten Thousand to Mesopotamia and back. His account illustrates many new features of contemporary arms and their use. That so large a force of Greek mercenaries could be raised, merely to support what proved to be the claim of a pretender to the Persian throne, is itself a sign of the times. That most of these were hoplites, and that they should again rout the opposing Oriental troops in the set battle at Cunaxa, was less novel. But their subsequent experiences were greatly varied. The missile-troops saved the force more than once. Among their number was a group of Rhodians (*Anabasis* III, 3, 16) who were skilled slingers although they had not enlisted in this capacity. By improvisation, slings and leaden bullets were made from local raw materials, and thereafter the Rhodians were able to outrange the enemy missile-troops, including even most of the archers. The Cretan archers in the Greek army had a different experience, being outranged by the Persians; but as Xenophon tells us in an interesting passage (III, 4, 17), 'the Persians use large bows, and so all the arrows of theirs which were picked up came in useful to the Cretans, who . . . practised long-range shooting with a high trajectory'. This implies or suggests several things, principally that the Cretan bow was also large, and perhaps that their arrows, with the large head of the Cretan type (pp. 40, 81), were heavier than the Persians' and so had a shorter range. It also strengthens the grounds for thinking that the Cretans used the more flexible composite bow, as the Persians certainly did. Xenophon's men also improvised a tiny cavalry force, using animals which had been carrying baggage, and fitting themselves out with leather jerkins; here again there is a contrast with the Persian cavalry, whose horses were evidently powerful enough to be armoured (I, 8, 7) and who were already masters of such skills as the 'Parthian shot' over the back of the saddle (III, 3, 10). In the mountains north of Mesopotamia, the Greeks were faced with what was virtually a long-bow, wielded by tribesmen who used their left foot as a fulcrum when drawing it, and shot huge armour-piercing arrows, so heavy that the Greeks were able to fit loops to them and return them as javelins (IV, 2, 28). About all arms except heavy infantry the Greeks still had much to learn, and not only from the civilized peoples. Later still in the march northwards they encountered the Chalybes of north-eastern Asia Minor, whose arms are described: linen corslet reaching down to the groin, greaves, helmet and a knife of about the size of a Spartan *xuēlē*—a weapon whose exact appearance is unknown (IV, 7, 16). The Chalybes must therefore be added to the list of barbarian peoples influenced by the armature of the Greek hoplite.

To a later period of Xenophon's career belong his other works which are relevant here: in particular, the masterly *On Horsemanship*, which at last gives a contemporary Greek view of a branch of warfare, including the appropriate arms for it (chapter

XII). Xenophon's prescriptions show that even now cavalry equipment was far from standardized: he recommends the problematical Boeotian helmet (p. 94); a corslet which would not impede the wearer from sitting down or raising his arms— the standard type with shoulder-pieces and *pteruges* (pp. 90-2) would fill this requirement, but Xenophon also prescribes a neck-guard or gorget, which is very rarely seen in art; and two offensive weapons probably borrowed from the Persians, a pair of javelins with cornel-wood shafts (*palta*) and a *kopis*, probably of the curved type described earlier (p. 97) which would make a good cavalry sabre. For the left arm, which must hold the reins, he prescribes a new piece of armour, the so-called 'hand' (*cheir*), a long tube apparently of leather construction which could be expanded to reach from the shoulder to the fingers, and which is portrayed on a much later Pergamene monument. For the right arm, Xenophon seems to recommend a rerebrace or vambrace of the old pattern (p. 93). The horse, significantly, is now to be armoured as well as the rider, most notably with the apron-like *parapleuridia*, which also protected the horseman's thighs. But Xenophon still prefers the cavalry to fight at long range— perhaps remembering a reverse in a minor cavalry engagement which he himself had witnessed in 396 (*Hellenica* III, 4, 13). His picture is, in general, a pessimistic one, and at other points in his writings there is more than a suggestion that the cavalryman's main preoccupation was to keep his seat. Yet a very different picture is given by the rather earlier grave-stelai of Attic cavalry-men which show the deceased man triumphant in battle; some are artistically superb, but all must observe some unrealistic conventions, of which the scanty clothing of the combatants is the most obvious.[22] Pl. 55

Xenophon had indeed lived on into an age of widespread reappraisal of war-methods. Infantry, even hoplites, and even in Sparta, were now becoming more mobile and less heavily armed. Already in 401, when the Ten Thousand parade before Cyrus (*Anabasis* I, 2, 16), the equipment of the hoplites is described, but there is no mention of the corslet; elsewhere in the work we hear of the *spolas*, a light cloth jerkin, being worn (III, 3, 20; IV, 1, 18).

The metal greave also appears to fade out of the picture at this time, although there are stray survivals in Greece and beyond. One reason for this was no doubt the increased prestige of the peltast; well before the end of the Peloponnesian War, Thrasyllus had organized and armed a peltast force from among the Athenians themselves, and there are also fragmentary Attic inscriptions dating to 416 and 415 which refer to peltasts.[23] Some years later we see the Athenian Iphicrates, a well-known mercenary commander, introducing what looks like the first directly antihoplite reform, if we can trust our rather poor sources (Diodorus XV, 44; Nepos, *Iphicrates* I). Not only did he train his men as peltasts, but he converted hoplites at least half-way to peltasts by withdrawing their great bronze shields and replacing them with lightweight oval ones. The final effects were dramatic: Arcadian hoplites would not even face Iphicrates' men (*Hellenica* IV, 4, 16), and in 390 he defeated a Spartan phalanx at Corinth. The adoption of his methods by other Greeks may even have led to the temporary eclipse of the original 'peltasts', the Thracians. An intermediate stage in the lightening of armour was the retention of the breastplate only, the 'half-corslet' or *hemithorakion*: it is first mentioned in an anecdote of Plutarch relating to the year 379, and it recurs in the next century (p. 125 below). The second-century AD lexicographer Pollux of Naucratis tells us that it was a device invented by Jason of Pherae in Thessaly, a briefly dominant figure in Greek warfare whose huge army—strong not only in the traditional Thessalian cavalry but in hoplites and particularly peltasts, and backed by mercenaries—appears suddenly in the pages of Xenophon without explanation of its origins. (We may note, however, that Thessalian hoplites were already serving in the Ten Thousand in 401). Jason further appears as the deviser of what sounds a very sophisticated formation for cavalry and light infantry in combination.[24]

Throughout the fourth century, the growth of mercenary service, and so of professionalism, is almost synonymous with the eclipse of the hoplite. The hoplite, who could afford to arm himself as few mercenaries or their employers could, yet remained as he had begun, primarily a citizen soldier and essentially an amateur. Even in Sparta, where agriculture was in the hands of the Helots and the hoplite was left free for intensive training and continuous service, the inhibiting attitudes and tactics of the phalanx placed a distinct advantage in the hands of an enterprising enemy who was bound by no old-fashioned code. The 600 Spartan hoplites found this to their cost when attacked by Iphicrates and his mercenaries under the walls of Corinth in 390 (Xenophon, *Hellenica* IV, 5, 14–17); but there were more and more commanders who were following Iphicrates in questioning the hallowed assumptions and priorities of warfare. The one great exception to this tendency is Epaminondas of Thebes, a thoughtful soldier who yet preferred to operate with the traditional hoplite methods, and indeed made his chosen instrument the Sacred Band of 300 hoplites. His prime contribution was in tactics: he drew up the *left* wing of his phalanx in great depth (fifty ranks at Leuctra) with the Sacred Band in front, and drove this wedge through the enemy's right, traditionally the strongest part of the phalanx. This apparently simple expedient had nevertheless had to wait until the declining years of the hoplite before being put into practice; its effect, backed by the skilled handling of cavalry, was the unique feat of overcoming the Spartan phalanx in full-scale battles twice in a decade.

In many reforms of this period, particularly those concerned with cavalry, we may discern that the pacemakers were once again the Greeks of Sicily, now largely under the domination of Dionysius I of Syracuse. Dionysius was one of the great pioneers of siege-warfare, with which we are not here concerned, but not to the exclusion of other arms. His preparations for his great war against Carthage make formidable reading: according to Diodorus (XIV, 43, 2–3), equipment was prepared for no less than 140,000 infantrymen, probably light-armed, and 14,000 cavalry. All Syracuse rang with the armourers' work. The cavalry were fitted with specially elaborate cuirasses, evidently largely metal, which with the vast over-all numbers speaks eloquently for the wealth and ascendancy of the western Greeks. This was illustrated a generation later when Dionysius, still in power, sent a force of his picked Gallic and Iberian mercenaries, as well as fifty Syracusan horsemen, to the aid of Sparta.[25] The virtuosity of these troops, and particularly of the tiny cavalry force, was a revelation to the Greeks of the homeland, notwithstanding that Greece herself had by now produced in Pelopidas of Thebes her first outstanding cavalry commander. Everywhere the old pattern was breaking up; the stage was set for a sweeping and positive military reform which might finally displace the hoplite as the backbone of Greek armies.

To us, looking back over 150 years of Classical warfare, it certainly appears that the Greeks of the homeland were timid and reactionary in their war-craft, clinging as they did to a military instrument which was already old when this period began. The moment of truth, which came to the hoplite at the hands of the Macedonian phalanx and cavalry at Chaeronea in 338, would seem to have been long overdue. But we should never forget that we are dealing with a people who, however frequently they fought, still regarded warfare as a deplorable incursion into their political and social life, which should be curtailed as far as possible. The aptness of hoplite warfare to this attitude had long since been discovered in internal struggles, before the Persian Wars proved that it was also, in certain given situations, a highly effective military method. Thereafter, Greece could reasonably hope not to have to defend her freedom against invaders, as indeed for long proved to be the case, while for internal wars the old methods were as acceptable as ever to either side. All in all, it is hard to see more than two ways in which the course of events could have been altered or accelerated: the Persians, or a yet more formidable aggressor than they, might have conquered or heavily defeated hoplite Greece—but the Assyrians, the likeliest possibility, were themselves mercifully extinguished too early for this to happen; or the growth of mercenary professionalism could have ended the indispensability of the hoplite to his city. This latter development was indeed on the way to becoming a reality, when Macedon at last transformed the military scene.

But our knowledge of warfare in mainland Greece should never be applied uncritically to the far less well-documented outlying areas of the Greek world. The experience of Ionia, for example, was far different, and to a great extent involved the first of the two alternatives suggested above. After the early period we hear comparatively little of the hoplite there, in either political or military history, and it is a fact that many Ionian cities were forced to accept Persian, and before that Lydian, dominion. Possibly the hoplite system had partly broken down in the rather different pattern of siege and naval warfare which seems to have been the Ionians' lot. If so, this did not apparently lead to any great military advance or innovation. In the far west, on the other hand, the Greeks of Sicily again and again show their independence of mind and ability to think beyond the set-piece tactics of the phalanx, particularly in the realms of cavalry and siege-warfare. Possibly the fact that most of their cities were founded before the hoplite system had caught on in Greece had something to do with it. While hoplite Greece was approaching the ultimate débâcle in the war against Macedon, her Sicilian kinsmen under Timoleon were saving their liberty against great odds at the Crimisus. We know little of Timoleon's army beyond its small number (12,000), but it included 3000 citizens of Syracuse, probably hoplites, besides mercenaries from the Greek homeland, among whom were Phocian peltasts and Corinthian hoplites. His Carthaginian enemies, too, are described as fighting in a phalanx, and were at least as well-armed, since after the battle no less than 1000 corslets and 10,000 shields are said to have been brought to Timoleon's tent.[26] It is sad that, among surviving authors, the great feats of arms in the west had no adequate historian to describe them.

CHAPTER V

MACEDON

PHILIP II and his son Alexander raised Macedonia, in the space of thirty years, from a precarious kingdom on the fringes of the Greek world, to the conqueror both of Greece and of her greatest enemy, the Persian empire. Of the military instruments by which this was achieved, we know, on the human and the tactical side, a good deal; but of arms and equipment we have a most defective picture. The Macedonians, it is true, did occasionally bury soldiers with their weapons, like other peoples in the outlying parts of Greece. But finds of armour are rare, and with representational vase-painting now moribund in mainland Greece, we have to depend largely on coins, grave-stelai and other relief-sculpture for artistic evidence. These, supplemented by inscriptions and detailed written accounts, are perhaps just enough.

The general outline is sufficiently clear.[1] Macedonia was traditionally cavalry country; we may recall the exploits, narrated by Xenophon (*Hellenica* V, 2–3), of Derdas of Elimia and his horsemen, with whom contemporary Greek cavalry could evidently not compete. The old aristocratic mounted retinue of the king was converted under Alexander into a small but vital striking force, the Companion cavalry, about 2000 strong. These were the main heavy cavalry and, as we shall see, ideas as to how much armour a horseman should wear had developed considerably. The more numerous light cavalry, some of them Paeonians, Thracians and Thessalians, were also important, but a force of probably Macedonian lancers, the *Sarissophoroi*, were a speciality of Alexander's and are seen neither earlier nor later.

For infantry, the poor and scattered peasant population of Macedonia could not be expected to arm itself to the standard of the Greek hoplite, and it did not attempt to. Instead it was turned, certainly by Philip II's time and conceivably even earlier, into an instrument that was altogether new, although its name— the phalanx—was a word as old as Homer. This was the most important innovation of the Macedonian reform; its use, in Alexander's hands, may be compared with that of an anvil rather than a hammer. Its members were honoured with the name 'Foot-Companions' on the model of the heavy cavalry. Their weapon was a huge pike, the *sarissa*. Tactically, the cavalry on the wings and the slower-moving phalanx in the centre were linked by bodies of troops called hypaspists. Whatever the original significance of their name—shield-bearers or squires to the cavalry perhaps—it had ceased to correspond with their function. Nor were they light-armed troops in the traditional sense, as some have suggested; their place in the main battle-line is a proof of this, and there is no record of their having thrown their spears or other weapons. Their differences from the Foot-Companions of the phalanx were mainly tactical, and their armament, never explicitly distinguished by our ancient sources, may have been almost identical. The true light-armed forces were missile-troops on the old pattern, javelin-throwers and archers—the latter were inevitably Cretans, while the javelin-men were partly Thracians and partly Agrianes from the mountains north of Macedonia, a new and potent source of fighting-men, who also served as slingers. A corps of slingers already existed under Philip II, as we shall see. Philip and Alexander also used mercenary troops, but not on the vast scale of their successors, so that in essentials, theirs was still a Macedonian national army.[2]

What sort of arms had been in use by the traditional Macedonian cavalry-forces before this? We have little material for the long period between the Dark Age cemeteries at Verghina and elsewhere and the rise of Philip. From Thucydides (II, 100, 4) we learn that in 429 the already redoubtable Macedonian horsemen were armoured with corslets. This seems to be contradicted by the evidence of occasional Macedonian coins, some of even earlier date, but this is probably because coin-engravers, like sculptors, cannot be expected to put realism before aesthetic effect. On helmets there is rather better evidence: as if following Xenophon's advice about all-round vision, the Macedonians had adopted more than one of the Greek open-faced varieties. The 'Illyrian' type is worn by some fifth- and fourth-century kings on their coins; rather later, we see the Thracian helmet, accepted farther south in the mid-fifth century, appearing in some of its many forms in Macedonia. From a fourth-century grave near Salonika comes a fine example of the 'Chalcidian' type, now in the British Museum, while Seleucus I chose to be portrayed on his coins wearing the Attic type.[3] Whether Macedonia ever acquired even a small hoplite force is questionable. King Perdiccas in 424 was evidently paying half the keep of Brasidas' Spartans while they were in his country, and the habit of hiring Greek hoplite mercenaries seems still to have been practised by Philip's father Amyntas. Thucydides does tell us (II, 100, 1) that Archelaus, the son of Perdiccas (413–399) improved the armament of his troops, but this need not imply that they were hoplites. Philip himself learned the arts of war under the most masterly of all hoplite commanders, Epaminondas of Thebes, to whom he had been sent as a hostage; but his assumption of power in 359 soon made obsolete nearly everything that had gone before. *Pls. 49, 59, 60*

The first archaeological trace of Philip's handiwork is provided by the city of Olynthus, which became his victim by capture in 348. The careful American excavations of this luxuriously laid-out town and its suburbs have yielded what is easily the best evidence for missile-warfare in Greek history. We are not primarily concerned here with the siege-artillery, in the use of which Philip had considerably developed the work of Dionysius of Syracuse. In Greece proper, by contrast, this field of warfare had been rather neglected, although a fine bronze battering-ram dating from fully a century before this has turned up at Olympia; Pericles is said to have used rams and other siege-engines at Samos in 440 (Diodorus XII, 28, from Ephorus), and Athens possessed catapults of a simple kind by the mid-fourth century. But even Philip had only the arrow-firing catapult, like a giant bow on its side, at Olynthus; the more powerful stone-throwing torsion catapult was probably first used in the time of Alexander. One very large type of 'arrowhead' found at Olynthus may very well come from the bolts fired by Philip's catapults; the heads are bronze and up to three inches long, a greatly enlarged version of the type of Scythian head with three barbs, and were inscribed at the time of casting with the legend 'PHILIPPO(U)'. But there were also masses of arrowheads of normal size. Commonest was the Scythian form with three fins (but no barbs), but there were also many of the large tanged 'Cretan' heads (p. 81), a possible sign that Philip already had Cretan archers. There were also found some long tanged arrowheads of square section, in iron, originally a Cypriote form, but known in Greece since the Persian Wars, and in Crete from much earlier. A number of cruder iron heads also occurred, such as were often produced in Classical Greece when large numbers of arrows were needed. *Sarissa-* and javelin-heads, and butt-spikes of both bronze and iron, were also present. Finally there were the lead sling-bullets, roughly almond-shaped and often inscribed, some with the names of Philip or his officers, others with sardonic slogans—'a nasty present', and the like. Both sides used the sling, the Macedonian bullets averaging about 30 grammes to the Olynthians' about 20. Of the defenders one other symbolic relic was found—an old-fashioned hoplite shield; after well over three centuries of existence, the bronze *hoplon* is still virtually unchanged in form, and retains the multiple cable-pattern round the rim.[4]

For the arms of the other Macedonian troops, we have to rely mainly on representations. To take the infantry first, it seems that neither the men of the phalanx nor the hypaspists now wore corslets; at least there is no positive evidence that they did, while their mobility in pursuit, the precedent of Xenophon's Ten Thousand, and the evidence of one or two inscriptions all argue against the possibility. They were thus in no real sense heavy infantry. Indeed Alexander, by his handling of them in his campaigns, at times appears to treat them as even lighter-armed troops than his Greek peltasts. They did however wear metal helmet and greaves, and carried a bronze-faced shield of much reduced dimensions. The later writer on tactics, Asclepiodotus (V, 1), gives the diameter of the Macedonian shield as eight palms (about two feet) and describes it as 'not too concave'. It was probably handled by the age-old means of a strap running round the neck, perhaps supplemented by a central handle for the elbow so as to leave both hands free; it could thus be slung over one's back when on the march. The shields of the hypaspists appear to be specially stressed, and could carry as a device a star. In later times there are a number of references to élite corps of infantry called 'Silver Shields', 'White Shields' and 'Bronze Shields'; whether or not these are the true descendants of Alexander's hypaspists is doubtful. The regular helmet, whether for infantry or cavalry, seems to have been of the Thracian type, which had now developed into a high-crowned affair, often with a flowing crest.[5]

The dominant offensive weapon of the age, carried by some of the cavalry as well as the men in the phalanx (p. 114), is of course the *sarissa*. About its dimensions and exact use, our sources disagree and learned argument has long been rife.[6] The two best, because contemporary, authorities are, for the fourth century, Theophrastus who in his *History of Plants* (III, 12, 2) says that the longest *sarissae* are 12 cubits (18 feet); and for the second century Polybius, who tells us that an original design with a length of 16 cubits had been abandoned in favour of one of 14 cubits (21 feet), which was now standard (XVIII, 29, 2). Both authors may be trusted to speak accurately of their own times, and they need not quite contradict each other; one or other of their figures for length, and one or two more besides, are quoted by other writers. The proposal to take 'cubits' in these passages as a mistake for 'feet', on the ground that the weapon is impossibly big for the cavalry *Sarissophoroi*, is unjustified. Polybius goes on to explain how the phalanx used this weapon; they grasped it in both hands, and from the left (front) hand to the butt of the shaft was 6 feet. There was thus a free projection of 15 feet, and since the ranks stood 3 feet apart, it is clear that only the weapons of the front five ranks could be used offensively. The remainder—the Macedonian phalanx usually had sixteen ranks—could offer only their weight, and the protection against missiles afforded by holding their *sarissae* over the heads of the front ranks. The great length of the weapon also posed the problem of balance. Here the most apt suggestion is that the wooden shaft, probably of ash, tapered strongly from butt to tip; it evidently lacked a butt-spike. For this same reason, the metal head will not have been large, and we can probably recognize as *sarissa*-heads many of the moderate-sized iron examples from Olynthus and from Macedonian cemetery-sites. The medieval Swiss pike provides several analogies with the *sarissa*. The other main problem about the *sarissa*, namely whether the front ranks of the phalanx had weapons of different lengths, graded so as to present a single wall of spearheads at one point, need not concern us here. Different authors—and in some cases the same author—tell us different things, and it would seem most reasonable to conclude that practices varied. Of the other weapons of the infantry we hear little. The hypaspists presumably had a shorter spear, and the Thracian light-armed carried a very large weapon called the *rhomphaia* (in Latin also *rumpia*, used by Livy of the Thracians (XXXI, 39, 11) and elsewhere), whose identification is extremely difficult. All the infantry carried swords, primarily for stabbing and of moderate size; in this respect they were at a serious disadvantage against the Roman legionaries, who, under the influence of the Celtic peoples, had adopted a heavy cutting-sword as a primary weapon. The 'Spanish sword' of the Romans made so strong an impact on the Macedonians as to affect the final outcome of the struggle between the two peoples. But the curved Greek *kopis* still had its uses at Macedon, as the mosaic of the lion-hunt from Pella shows.[7]

The lightening of the infantry's armour was more than matched by the increase in that of the cavalry. Earlier Macedon had given a foretaste of this (p. 115), but now the standard equipment of the Companions embraced metal corslet and helmet, spear and sword. The last was probably in the form of the *kopis*, as pre-scribed by Xenophon; with this weapon, according to Arrian's version at least (I, 15, 8), Clitus sheared off at a blow the arm and shoulder of a Persian who was threatening Alexander in the fighting at the Granicus. To judge from fourth-century coins, the standard corslet was the close-fitting plated 'muscle-cuirass' (p. 92). But the slightly older form with shoulder-flaps was also in use, and it is this that Alexander is wearing in the famous mosaic of the battle of Issus from Herculaneum, a copy of an almost contemporary work. At Gaugamela, on the other hand, he had an elaborate linen corslet, captured from the Persians. We are not told which type it was that was later pierced by an Indian arrow in the siege of the city of the Malli. Whether or not Alexander went into the battle of Issus bare-headed as the mosaic suggests, it was as well that he did not do so at Granicus, where he received a heavy blow on the helmet. In any case, the normal practice of the Companions was to wear helmets usually of Thracian type; Alexander had an unusual iron one at Gaugamela. Their opponents, the Persian cavalry, as in Xenophon's day, were heavily armoured. The spear of the Companion cavalry was of moderate length compared with that of the *Sarissophoroi*, and carried a spear-butt as well as a head; it was probably what Xenophon and some later writers called the *xyston*. The artists and the more reliable authors suggest that at the time of Alexander's wars the cavalry carried no shield. Alexander himself made experiments with mounted javelin-throwers and archers, but they were not really characteristic of his time.[8] It is a fair summary to say that he won his victories over the Persians without the clear superiority in arms and armour which the fifth-century Greeks had enjoyed.

Alexander's methods in war can be clearly distinguished from those of his successors, most obviously in questions of tactics, but also in arms and equipment. The salient fact is the gradual neglect of cavalry, typified by the seeming disappearance of the Companions and *Sarissophoroi*, and the concentration on, and greater specialization of, the phalanx. Man-power difficulties in the far-flung kingdoms of the Diadochi may well lie at the root of this; phalangites might be trained from among non-Macedonians more easily than heavy cavalry. These processes seem to have run their course in the long and comparatively obscure period between the battles of Ipsus (301) and Sellasia (222); by the latter date they had affected the arms of infantry and cavalry alike. To the third century no doubt belong the experiments in lengthening the original 18-foot *sarissa* (p. 118). The names of the new infantry-corps of this period (*ibid.*) suggest that the shield

58 Two views of the Boeotian type of helmet recommended by Xenophon for cavalry use, as offering the least obstruction to the vision and hearing of the wearer. This example was found in the River Tigris, which indicates how far afield the type was adopted. See pp. 94, 125.

59-60 *Left:* Obverse of a stater of Eucratides I of Bactria (180-150 BC). This Hellenistic king is wearing a late form of the Boeotian helmet, shown here with a crest-plume. See p. 125. *Right, above and below:* Obverse and reverse of a tetradrachm of Seleucus I (306-280 BC), one of the most able of the generals of Alexander the Great. He is shown on the obverse wearing an Attic helmet, and the reverse shows the goddess Niké crowning a trophy of arms. See p. 116.

was now emphasized, but in the phalanx at least it can hardly have become bigger, since the close-order (*synaspismos*) whereby each man was allegedly given a frontage of only 18 inches was adhered to in many Hellenistic armies.[9] Some Hellenistic troops, both in Greece and farther east, are described as 'cuirassiers' (*thorakitai*) by Polybius (IV, 12, 3; X, 29, 6; XI, 11, 5); but these men are evidently not part of the phalanx proper. One interesting sidelight on the later development of the phalanx is given by the description of Antiochus IV's great review of his troops at Daphne in 165, where there appears a force of 5000 men 'armed in the Roman fashion with corslets of chain-armour' (XXX, 25, 3). This was perhaps a posthumous reaction to the verdict of Pydna and the earlier battles; the size of Antiochus' phalanx (over 30,000, including the 'Roman-armed') is also exceptionally large for the Seleucid army.

The Macedonian type of phalanx could be just as clumsy on rough ground as the hoplite one (*cf.* Polybius XI, 15–16), but this did not prevent it from dominating warfare to an ever-increasing degree. The descriptions of Hellenistic armies show how this tendency developed. Whereas Eumenes of Cardia, in the best tradition of his master Alexander, was able to defeat Craterus in Cappadocia in 321, although utterly outclassed in the phalanx, by a successful charge with both wings of his stronger cavalry (Diodorus XVIII, 30), a century later this feat would scarcely have been attempted. Perhaps the best example is provided by a battle of which Polybius' detailed account has survived (V, 65 and 79–84), Raphia in 217. Here two huge armies, both seeking battle, faced each other on the flat plains north of Sinai which have since witnessed several bold cavalry campaigns; but these armies were both more than 90 per cent infantry. Ptolemy IV, the eventual victor, was no military genius; he was outnumbered both in cavalry and light-armed troops, and his 73 small African elephants were inferior in both number and quality to the Indian ones of his opponent, the able but inexperienced Antiochus. But his vast phalanx—altogether some 48,000 men armed 'in the Macedonian manner' if Polybius' figures are correct[10]—proved too strong for the smaller Seleucid one. The local successes of

Antiochus' right wing and elephants, and of Ptolemy's own right, had no effect on the infantry struggle. No one seems to have thought of rolling up the line from the flank, and the turning-point of the battle came when Ptolemy abandoned his defeated left and joined the phalanx.

The most significant ratio within an army, that of phalanx to cavalry, had also changed radically. Alexander had kept it within the region of 2 to 1, and at Ipsus there was still adequate pro-vision of cavalry on both sides, but at Raphia Antiochus had 5 to 1, and Ptolemy at least 5 and perhaps nearly 10 to 1. The later Macedonian kings showed an equal or even greater obsession with the phalanx: Antigonus Doson had a ratio of 8 to 1 at Sellasia, Philip V preserved 8 to 1 at Cynoscephalae and, though Perseus had more cavalry at Pydna, it proved of insignificant value. Yet Philip at least had shown himself earlier in his reign, at Lissus, (Polybius VIII, 14) as a masterly handler of peltasts and other light-armed troops.

Cavalry had meanwhile become more encumbered with armour. Polybius, whose account provides the first direct com-parison between Greek arms and Roman (VI, 25), relates that the Roman cavalry modelled their equipment on that of the Greeks, to the extent of wearing corslets and adopting stout spears with butt-spikes. From this passage we also learn that the cavalry of Hellenistic Greece had begun, perhaps in the third century, to carry shields. Polybius describes them as firm and stout. They seem to have been of some considerable size, round and at times faced with bronze, for an actual example was excavated at Pergamon, and the Roman monument commemorating the battle of Pydna shows Macedonian cavalry with more ornate but otherwise similar shields. For body-armour, a kind of hybrid had earlier been formed of the two main corslet-types of Classical Greece, plated like the 'muscle-cuirass' but with the shoulder-flaps coming over to fasten in the front; this reappears on a Pergamene relief. From the same source we learn that the Thracian helmet was still in vogue in Hellenistic times; indeed, there is an example from northern Macedonia in Berlin, inscribed with the name of Monunios, a king of the Illyrians in the first half of the third century.[11] Plutarch's life of Demetrius the Besieger (XXI) mentions, in connection with the siege of Rhodes in 305-4, that an Epirot officer in Demetrius' army wore a corslet that weighed two talents, which should be about a hundredweight. Other examples of half that weight are mentioned, while Demetrius himself is considered to have an unusually light outfit when he receives two Cypriot iron corslets weighing rather less than forty pounds each. These last were presumably scale-corslets; detached iron scales are found from the Archaic period in Cyprus, although iron as a defensive material is very rare in earlier Greek history. One suspects that such armour as this must have been worn when on horseback, and the tendency from the fourth century on is certainly away from heavy body-armour for infantry; nevertheless, officers still often wore corslets even among the infantry. While we are on the subject of heavy cavalry it would be a pity to omit all mention of its apotheosis, the war-elephant, whose golden age falls in the third century BC. But it was tactical considerations which determined the rise and fall of the elephant as a war-arm; the thickness of its skin placed it beyond the reach of mere improvements in arms and armour. *Pl. 57*

The functions of the light-armed troops were not greatly augmented within the Hellenistic period. It is true that we are often hampered by the confusions of our sources, most of whom were not contemporary with the events they describe. Nor are matters improved by translation into Latin terminology: Livy's *caetrati*, for example, is a term which he uses to mean peltasts; but at times it seems to be applied to troops armed with the thrusting-spear and even fighting in the phalanx (XLIV, 41, 2 and 9). Even in Polybius, there are 'peltasts' who are described as being among the more heavily-armed troops (*e.g.* V, 23, 3), which has led to the suggestion that he is referring to the hypaspists, otherwise so mysteriously almost absent from the descriptions of armies after Alexander.[12] The true peltasts now carried the oval or oblong shield called the *thureos*, at least as commonly as the *pelta*. The Thracians were still often conspicuous in this department; at Pydna, they appear armed with long shields and greaves, as well as the enigmatic *rhomphaia* (p. 119 and note 7).

Missile-troops, though seldom prominent in the accounts of Hellenistic battles, did undergo further development. In particular the function of the slinger was extended by the *cestrosphendonē*, a Macedonian invention of about 170, whereby a short iron bolt, fitted to a slightly longer wooden shaft with flights attached, was propelled by a sling with two loops; it must have been formidable at short range. Another comparable device, which perhaps comes rather under the heading of siege-artillery, was a sling mounted on a long pole and wielded by the ordinary foot-soldier, which projected large stones to a much increased range. Archery remained a flourishing activity, with Cretan mercenaries playing as prominent a part as ever. An interesting illustration of this is given by a group of arrowheads of the Cretan type, on which is incised a monogram formed of the letters B and E—an abbreviation, as coin-parallels show, for Berenice, and perhaps commemorating the wife of Ptolemy III (247–222). Examples have been found at Knossos (on whose coins the plain version of this arrowhead had appeared in the fourth century), and also in Egypt, Byblos and Cyrene; one example, in the British Museum, is even said to have been found in the River Kennet near Reading, though if so it was probably a modern loss. Plain specimens also occur in Syria and Palestine at this time. But for archery as for cavalry, the battle of Magnesia in 190 must have proved a setback. Antiochus the Great, in a belated reversion to something resembling the methods of Alexander, staked his main hopes not on the phalanx but on a striking force of Persian cavalry, and also put into the field a motley horde of Cretan and other archers, some of them mounted on horses, camels and elephants. But notwithstanding the assistance of Hannibal, the success of the cavalry, and his numerical superiority of more than two to one over the Romans, Antiochus lost decisively. Some Cretan troops had earlier appeared in Antiochus' army in an unfamiliar guise, armed with shields and providing cover for the missile-troops,[13] but it is as archers that the Cretans still occur all over the Hellenistic world, including Pontus, Syracuse and Rome.

The mention of Cretans raises the question of arms in Greece outside Macedonia and its sphere of influence. Developments had not always followed the same pattern here. Greek mercenary peltasts and, more rarely, hoplites were worth hiring in Alexander's time, and remained so until at the Peace of Apamea in 188 Rome put a sharp check on their recruitment. The triumphs of Boeotian hoplite infantry down to the death of Epaminondas in 362 had not been forgotten, and the Greek hoplite lived to fight many another day. Even Philip's victory at Chaeronea could be ascribed more to his generalship, particularly the holding back of his right wing at the moment of impact, than to any innate superiority of the Macedonian phalangite to the Greek hoplite—indeed, the real heroes of the battle were the Theban Sacred Band. Seven years later, Agis III and his Spartan hoplites fought long and bravely against Antipater's phalanx at Megalopolis (Diodorus XVII, 63). But armour had now become much lighter; we see and hear little of the infantry corslet, although a treaty of about 270 between the Aetolians and the Acarnanians divides the infantry into panoply-wearers, 'half-corslet' wearers (see p. 110) and those without armour. Perhaps these remoter peoples of Greece, who had long hesitated to adopt hoplite equipment, were now slow in discarding it. The Corinthian helmet had long since disappeared from Greece proper, and the light Boeotian type was now favoured for infantry as well as cavalry, and well beyond Boeotia. In Hellenistic times it underwent some odd modifications. One of the very few actual examples, in the Ashmolean Museum, was found in the River Tigris, a hint of the widespread use that still existed for purely Greek arms. Dedications in Greek sanctuaries are no longer plentiful. We know from the Temple Chronicle of the sanctuary of Athena at Lindos that the practice of dedicating one's own personal armour, as well as that of conquered enemies, was now usual, but the finds to illustrate this are largely lacking both there and elsewhere. Only at Dodona is there any quantity of finds of likely Hellenistic date that have been published; cheek-pieces, probably from Thracian helmets, are among them. The distinction in equipment between hoplite and peltast was probably becoming less and less clear-cut, and only the traditional 'Argive' shield for a time survived to recall the hoplite's past. Light-armed troops were certainly in the greater demand, and those Greeks who specialized in this field—the Phocians, the Aetolians, the Achaeans—provided a peltast élite for many a Hellenistic army. The mercenary peltast, unlike the citizen hoplite, had a bad press in Greek literature; already in Middle Comedy he was introduced to the stage in the character of braggart and raconteur, before Plautus' *Miles Gloriosus* perpetuated him.[14]

Of the greater hoplite powers, Athens had already allowed herself to become heavily dependent on mercenaries in the fourth century, and the poor showing of her hoplites at Chaeronea was no cause for wonder. The Boeotians had fought and died nobly there, but perhaps as a result seem never to have recovered their hoplite prowess (see p.127), while Sparta in the third century fell on evil times, from which she only made a partial and temporary recovery through her social revolution late in that century. But yet again, we can discern a different situation in Sicily, where the campaigns of Agathocles against the Carthaginians in the years around 300, scrappily described by Diodorus, nevertheless show an accomplished general in command of a better army that most Hellenistic states could boast. Diodorus speaks of a picked force of 1000 'hoplites' (XX, 11, 1), and to judge from the example of southern Italy (p. 128) it is just possible that he is using the term in its accurate and traditional sense. In the main Agathocles' was a mercenary army as we should now expect, in Sicily especially; these hoplites may have been hired, as the slingers, archers and other troops from Greece and Italy certainly were.

Missile-troops, in Greece as in Macedonia, were not neglected. At Athens, mid-fourth-century inscriptions list boxes of arrows; in 282 a Cretan coach is recorded as being employed to train Athenian archers, and this practice was continued through the third and second centuries as later inscriptions show. Sparta too had long since employed Cretans. Archery was indeed now acquiring the status of an educational discipline, and from all over Greece—the Cyclades, Thessaly, Thrace, Ionia—come inscriptions recording archery competitions. One of these, of the early third century from the island of Ceos, again names the price of the various weapons which are offered as prizes. For the winner there was a bow and quiver worth 15 drachmai; the second prize, a bow alone, has a value of 7 drachmai; while a spear alone rates only just over half a drachma, as compared with the higher figure of rather more than a century earlier (p. 107); helmet and shield, finally, are valued at 6 and 20 drachmai respectively. From Olbia in south Russia comes a stone recording the fact that one Anaxagoras had shot a distance of 282 *orguiai*—about 550 yards; this must have been a competition feat with a light arrow, and bears no relation to the tactical range of the Greek or even the Cretan bow.[15] Of other missile-troops, the slingers of Achaea had perhaps acquired the most fame; but in Achaea there were still changes to come.

We read of Cleomenes III of Sparta, one of the better soldiers of the second half of the third century, that he changed the armament of his Spartan hoplites by introducing the *sarissa* which, being held by both hands, also necessitated a change of shield from the 'Argive' to the Macedonian type. This measure at first recalls that of Iphicrates some 150 years earlier (p. 110); he too had lengthened the spears and swords of his men. But Cleomenes' conversion to a thorough-going Macedonian phalanx was a more drastic step, and his force put up a brave fight against its original, the phalanx of Antigonus, at Sellasia. This reform may have been paralleled and in part anticipated by a decision of the Boeotians to adopt the equipment of the Macedonian hypaspist, some time very soon after 250.[16] Other Greeks must have followed one or other of these courses, and the army of the Achaean League seems to have emulated both: first we read of units armed on the model of the Macedonian corps called the 'Bronze Shields' (p. 118), and of others who wear corslets (Polybius II, 65, 3; IV, 69, 5; V, 91, 7; IV, 12, 3); then later occurs the somewhat obscure reform of the whole Achaean army by Philopoemen, mentioned much earlier (p. 72). Of the two quite full accounts which we have of this, Plutarch's (in *Philopoemen* IX) represents it as an adoption of the true Macedonian phalanx armed with the *sarissa*; while Pausanias (VIII, 50, 1) describes it equally explicitly in terms of the time-honoured (and now obsolescent) Greek hoplite arms, with the Argive shield and the corslet specifically mentioned. Plutarch, often the more reliable, has the edge in plausibility here too, although even he brings in the discordant touch of a corslet. Certainly, by the mid-second century Polybius can write of Greek soldiers in general 'having difficulty in carrying their *sarissae*' on the march, just as if they were all Macedonian phalangites.[17]

In one part of the Greek world, southern Italy, the heavy infantryman seems to have remained a dominant force for longer than elsewhere. The plate-corslet and other items of the hoplite panoply, such as greaves and ankle-guards, were here in common use in the fourth century among both Greeks and Italians, and the latter had also the custom of burying warriors with full defensive panoply. The wall-paintings of Lucanian soldiers with horned helmets based on the 'Chalcidian' type, from a tomb at Paestum, show one local variety of this armament, while on roughly contemporary Italiote vases and other monuments, we see the developments that it had undergone at the hands of the Samnites and their neighbours. Most conspicuous is a new form of breastplate, small, bronze and of a trefoil shape, emphasized by the decoration of the surface with three contingent circles. We also see small square plates, worn with or without a bronze belt; these are perhaps the model for the *kardiophylax* ('heart-protector') of early Roman infantry, described by Polybius (VI, 23, 14). The old pattern of 'Argive' shield was also long retained; the heavy spear and javelin were in much the same form as before, and even the Corinthian helmet lives on, though in a grievously distorted form, reminiscent of the debased armour and anti-functional shapes cultivated at the end of the great Age of Plate, in the sixteenth century AD and later: the eye-holes of the helmet and the space between the cheek-pieces are now false, being merely engraved in outline on the outer surface, so that the helmet could be worn only on the back of the head. In a different field, that of light cavalry, the mercenaries of Tarentum must have excelled before their city became the 'unwarlike Tarentum' of Horace; for the name 'Tarantinoi' came to be applied throughout the Hellenistic world, and irrespective of race, to a kind of light cavalry, probably equipped with javelins. This use of an ethnic name to describe a type of soldier is a typical feature of Hellenistic warfare, but it is likely to have its origin in a real connection with Tarentum.[18]

It was on the plains of southern Italy, too, that the Macedonian phalanx achieved its greatest successes against Roman arms, though at proverbial cost, under King Pyrrhus of Epirus. But a century later the balance had swung inexorably the other way. There is perhaps no better place or moment to leave the subject of Greek arms than the battlefield of Pydna in 168 BC.[19] By now the Roman legionaries had met and worsted the Macedonian phalanx more than once, by forcing it to expose its vulnerable flank; this had happened in the great battles of Cynoscephalae and Magnesia, and it was to happen again now, after a long and hard fight. But the sight of the close-packed phalanx of the Macedonians, just before battle was joined, and its subsequent charge, were still something to chill the heart; the seasoned Roman commander, Aemilius Paullus, could never afterwards forget the dismay of those moments. This was by no means the last appearance of the Macedonian type of phalanx in history: Mithridates of Pontus was still putting one into the field against Sulla nearly a century later, before he too realized the superiority of Roman arms and methods:[20] but it was nevertheless a worthy finale for the last major creation of Greek arms and tactics.

Thirty years ago, the leading authority on Hellenistic military history wrote: 'There is a certain body of archaeological evidence throwing some light upon the arms and accoutrements of Hellenistic soldiers, but it is both difficult to collect (much of it is unpublished), and of a highly specialized interest. . . . It awaits (I hope) a more able pen than my own'.[21] The present writer can only echo this hope, for the collection and even the publication are largely still awaited, and they lie far outside the scope of this work. The dearth of archaeological evidence for this latest period of Greek warfare matches the lack of written sources for the earliest; the wheel has turned full circle. Elsewhere in this study, the reader may feel that the bringing together of these two main classes of evidence has been less of a correlation than a confrontation.

At times the pursuit of our main aim, to find out what was actually happening, has involved outright rejection of one or the other kind of testimony, and this may have seemed presumptuous; but one is likely to have got far nearer to the true picture in cases where there are the different kinds of evidence to set against each other, than where—as in the Hellenistic age—there is almost no critical check that one can apply, unless the writers contradict each other. It is unlikely that our impression of Hellenistic arms is as far from reality as, say, that of Mycenaean arms may be. But we live in an uncertain age, and it is perhaps fitting that we should find the wars of the past as baffling as those of the future.

SOURCES

GENERAL SOURCES

There is no general work which covers this whole subject adequately. For many of the particular topics of Greek arms and armour, the most detailed treatment is to be found in doctoral dissertations, presented at German universities and subsequently published. I give a list of these together now, not because they are all of equal value but because they are, I fear, equally difficult to find in any but the best-equipped library; for this reason, they will not be cited in detail in the notes.

Shields: M. Greger, *Schildformen und Schildschmuck bei den Griechen* (Erlangen, 1908)

Helmets: E. Kukahn, *Der griechische Helm* (Marburg-an-der-Lahn, 1936)

Weapons: A. Schaumberg, *Bogen und Bogenschützen bei den Griechen* (Erlangen, 1910) and A. Remouchamps, *Griechische Dolch- und Schwertformen* (Leiden, 1926)

Body-armour: A. Hagemann, *Griechische Panzerung* (Leipzig, 1919) W. Gaerte, *Die Beinschützwaffen der Griechen* (Dresden, 1920)

Chariots: E. von Mercklin, *Der Rennwagen in Griechenland* (Leipzig, 1909)

Light-armed troops: O. Lippelt, *Die griechischen Leichtbewaffneten bis auf Alexander den Grossen* (Jena, 1910)

MUSEUM CATALOGUES

A few collections of Greek arms and armour have been published, either separately or as part of a general catalogue of bronzes:

Athens: A. de Ridder, *Bronzes trouvés sur l'Acropole d'Athènes* (1896)

Berlin: Staatliche Museen zu Berlin, *Führer durch das Antiquarium I,*
Bronzen (1924)
  Baron von Lipperheide, *Antike Helme* (a private collection, now
  in Berlin)
Karlsruhe: K. Schumacher, *Grossherzogliche vereinigte Sammlungen
zu Karlsruhe. Beschreibung der Sammlung antiker Bronzen* (1890)
London: H. B. Walters, *Catalogue of the Bronzes* (*Greek, Roman and
Etruscan*) *in the British Museum* (1899)
  Chapter VIII of *GRL* is also valuable.
New York: G. M. A. Richter, *Catalogue of the Greek, Roman and
Etruscan Bronzes in the Metropolitan Museum of Art* (1915)
Paris: A. de Ridder, *Bronzes Antiques du Louvre* I–II (1913–5)
  E. Babelon and A. Blanchet, *Catalogue des Bronzes, Bibliothèque
  Nationale* (1895)
St. Louis: T. T. Hoopes, *Arms and Armor* (1954)

SOURCES OF ILLUSTRATIONS

4, 15, 18, 20, 21, 22, 23, 27, 33, 55, Deutsches Archäologisches Institut,
Athens; 1, 2, 6, 7, 8, 9, 10, 36, 39, 47, Thames and Hudson Archives;
28, Edinburgh University photo; 26, courtesy Dr C. W. J. Eliot;
12, 57, photo Giraudon; 11, 56, National Museum, Athens; 5, 13,
École française d'Athènes; 3, British School of Archaeology in Athens;
59, Bibliothèque Nationale, Paris; 14, 25, 40, 58 a and b, Ashmolean
Museum; 16, 30, 37, photo Max Hirmer; 17, 24, 35, 49, from the
author's collection; 19, American School of Classical Studies in
Athens; 29, 48, 50, 51, 52, 54, British Museum; 31, 42, 43, 44, Soprint-
endenza dell'Antichitá, Palermo; 32, courtesy The Ephor of Anti-
quities, Heraklion; 34, National Museum, Copenhagen, photo
Lennart Larsen; 38, 53, Staatliche Museen, Berlin; 41, photo Edwin
Smith; 45, Kunsthistorische Museum, Vienna; 60 a and b, photo
Peter Clayton; 46, Metropolitan Museum, New York.

NOTES

ABBREVIATIONS

AA	*Archäologischer Anzeiger* (supplement to *JdI*)
AD	*Arkhaiologikon Deltion*
AE	*Arkhaiologikē Ephemeris*
AGA	D. von Bothmer, *Amazons in Greek Art* (1957)
AJA	*American Journal of Archaeology*
AM	*Mitteilungen des deutschen archäologishen Instituts, Athenische Abteilung*
AR	*Archaeological Reports* (supplement to *JHS*)
BCH	*Bulletin de Correspondance Hellénique*
BSA	*Annual of the British School at Athens*
Documents	M. G. F. Ventris and J. Chadwick, *Documents in Mycenaean Greek* (1956)
EGA	A. M. Snodgrass, *Early Greek Armour and Weapons* (1964)
GRL	British Museum, *Guide to the Exhibition of Greek and Roman Life*, 3rd ed. (1929)
HGVP	P. E. Arias, M. Hirmer and B. B. Shefton, *History of Greek Vase-painting* (1962)
HM	H. L. Lorimer, *Homer and the Monuments* (1950)
JdI	*Jahrbuch des deutschen archäologischen Instituts*
JHS	*Journal of Hellenic Studies*
Karo	G. Karo, *Die Schachtgräber von Mykenai* (1930)
Kromayer	J. Kromayer and G. Veith, *Heerwesen und Kriegführung der Griechen und Römer* (1928)
MA	*Monumenti Antichi* (Reale Accademia dei Lincei)
MHW	G. T. Griffith, *Mercenaries of the Hellenistic World* (1935)
Ol.	*Olympia, Ergebnisse der Ausgrabungen* I–V (1890–6)
Ol. ber.	*I–VII Bericht über die Ausgrabungen in Olympia* (1937–61)
Ol. Forsch.	*Olympische Forschungen* I–V (1944–64)

PCG   British Museum, *Guide to the Principal Coins of the Greeks*, 2nd ed. (1959).

PM   A. J. Evans, *The Palace of Minos* I–IV (1921–35)

SSG   G. M. A. Richter, *The Sculpture and Sculptors of the Greeks* (revised edition 1950)

CHAPTER I

1 The whole body of finds from the Shaft-graves is covered in Karo, *Die Schachtgräber*, although it was not possible to trace every object excavated by Schliemann. *HM*, chapter V, is still the best general survey of Mycenaean arms

2 Karo, pp. 200–6, type A, pls. 80–1, etc.: N. Sandars, *AJA* 1961, 17ff, pls. 15–17

3 Karo, type B, pl. 72, etc.: Sandars, *AJA* 1961, 22ff, pls. 18–19

4 *e.g.* Karo, pls. 89ff (daggers), 97 (choppers)

5 Karo, pls. 96, etc.: dagger-blade, pl. 94

6 *e.g.* Karo, pl. 97, no. 448

7 See *EGA* 245, note 3 for some examples of Mycenaean javelins; there are at least two further fresco-fragments which could be added to the list.

8 See W. E. McLeod's studies of Eygptian bows in *AJA* 1958, 397ff and 1962, 13ff; and for all Mycenaean arrowheads, H.-G. Buchholz' paper in *JdI* 1962, 1–58

9 See *HM* 276–80 on Mycenaean bows

10 Buchholz (above, note 8) 4ff, fig. 1

11 Karo, pls. 54–5

12 Linen, *AM* 1887, 21ff, fig. 4: gold bands, Karo pls. 67–8

13 Karo, pl. 70, nos. 541–9: compare a Minoan ivory, Zervos, *L'Art de la Crète* (1956), fig. 695

14 The best discussion of the boars' tusk helmet is in *HM* 212–19, although its length of life must now be extended (see note 43). For a reconstructed example, see A. J. B. Wace, *Chamber Tombs at Mycenae* (1932), pl. 38. Similarly 'built-up' helmets which may or may not be lined with boars' tusks are also frequent: *HM* 220–5, with figs. 2, 6, 7, 22 and pl. XV, 4

15 *HM* 134–46, figs. 1–8

16 *AE* 1957, parartema, 1–3

17 See G. E. Mylonas, *AJA* 1951, 134ff, for a sceptical view of this orthodox interpretation

18 See M. R. Popham, *AJA* 1964, 352: M. S. F. Hood, *Kadmos* 1965, 16–44

19 See N. Sandars, *AJA* 1963, 119–32, 144–9, types C and D, with pls. 21–3, 24. Both types are shown on Corsican megaliths, see *Antiquity* 1966, 193–8

20 *Documents* 360-1: J. Boardman, *On the Knossos Tablets* (1963), *79-80*
21 See especially *BSA* 1952, 255ff, with fig. 12 and pl. 53 b
22 Linear B tablet, *Documents* 361: another, and at times even larger spear-head was found at Thebes (*Illustrated London News*, 5/12/64, 896-7) and Knossos, *BSA* 1952, 261-2, fig. 8 ('AJ 3')
23 Sealings, *Documents* 361: other Armoury finds, *PM* IV, 832-41
24 *AE* 1957, parartema, 15-18: *AR* 1960-1, 9-10
25 See C. ffoulkes, *Armour and Weapons* (1909), pl. VIII, right
26 Swords, *AJA* 1963, 145, 148: 'helmet', A. W. Persson, *New Tombs at Dendra* (1943), 43, 119ff
27 Phaestos: *MA* 1904, 537ff and *BSA* 1952, 260-1: Thebes, *Illustrated London News*, 5/12/64, 896-7 and *AR* 1964-5, 15
28 *PM* IV, 803-6; *Documents* 379-81, with *BSA* 1957, 148-9 and 1962, 52 on corslets and helmets; also *Kadmos* 1965, 96-110
29 *BSA* 1952, 256ff, pls. 50-2
30 Vase with discs, *Antiquity* 1954, 211ff, pls. 8-9; Isopata and Hagia Triada, *HM* 220, fig. 22 and pl. XV, 5
31 *PM* III, 301-17
32 *Documents* 361-72
33 See H. W. Catling, *Cypriot Bronzework in the Mycenaean World* (1964), 294ff
34 Sandars (see note 19), 133-9, pl. 25, Type F; compare the rather more impressive type with hooked hand-guards, pl. 26, Type G
35 On *Griffzungenschwerter*, see Catling in *Proceedings of the Prehistoric Society* 1956, 107ff and *Antiquity* 1961, 115ff
36 On European spears in general, Sandars, 142-3: flame-shaped type, *EGA* 119, 208
37 For these Cypriot weapons, see Catling, *Cypriot Bronzework*, 117-25
38 Arrowheads, Buchholz (see note 8), especially type VII C: Iolkos vase, *BCH* 1961, 769, fig. 21: for examples of sling-bullets, see *PM* II, 345
39 See ffoulkes (see note 25), 97
40 *HM* 200-2, pl. III, 1 with associated monuments, fig. 9 and pls. II, 2 and XII, 1-2: Pylos tablets, *Documents* 375-9 and *Kadmos* 1965, 99-105
41 *AM* 1960, 43, 47, Beilage 29
42 Fresco, *HM* 251, pl. XII, 3: greaves and ankle-guard, *AM* 1960, Beilage 26, 3-5 and 28, and Catling, *Cypriot Bronzework*, 133ff
43 Kallithea, *AM* 1960, 44, Beilage 31, 4
44 *HM* 211, 225, pl. XIII, 1
45 *HM* 146-51, fig. 9 and pls. II-III
46 *EGA* 38-48
47 Chariot: tablets, *Documents* 372-5; representations, *e.g. HM* 314ff, figs. 44-5; cavalryman on vase, *HM* 154, fig. 10, and for latest dating V. R. d'A. Desborough, *The Last Mycenaeans and their Successors* (1964), 27, 177, 188

CHAPTER II

1 On early iron, see especially H. H. Coghlan, Pitt-Rivers Museum, *Occasional Papers on Technology*, no. 8 (1956), and D. H. F. Gray, *JHS* 1954, 1–16
2 See Desborough, *op. cit.* (Ch. I, note 47), 70, pl. 24 d, e
3 On early iron swords in the Aegean, *EGA* 93ff: on 'killing' of weapons, see L. V. Grinsell, *Folklore* 1961, 475ff
4 On early spears, *EGA* 115–36
5 J. K. Brock, *Fortetsa* (1957), 22, 202: other Cypriot types and practices, *EGA* 116, 120–2, 263 note 13 (but it was perhaps incorrect to say that these sockets were all forged)
6 *AD* 1963, 222 (Verghina)
7 *EGA* 136–9: add *AM* 1963, 35–40 (Gr. XXIII, Tiryns)
8 See *HM* 259–60
9 On Homer, *HM* 289–300: arrowheads, *EGA* 148, 155, 265 note 37, and add now two obsidian examples from a grave of about 900 at Tiryns, *AM* 1963, 41
10 On Homer and the composite bow, *HM* 276–7, 290–300
11 *EGA* 147–8
12 *HM* 276–89: for additions and corrections, *EGA* 141–3
13 *BCH* 1957, 340–56, pls. II–III
14 G. von Merhart in *Origines* (Como, 1954), 33–61: *EGA* 77–83
15 *HM* 246–7: École française d'Athènes, *Fouilles de Delphes* V (1908), 31–3, pl. 1
16 *BCH* 1958, 662, fig. 8: *AM* 1963, 17ff, fig. 9, Beilage 6–7
17 On early helmets and crests, *EGA* 5–13
18 Argos helmet, *BCH* 1957, 356–67 and *EGA* 13ff
19 Catling, *Cypriot Bronzework* 142ff: bosses in general, *EGA* 38ff
20 *HM* 156–67: T. B. L. Webster, *From Mycenae to Homer* (1958), 169ff: *EGA* 58ff
21 Aristotle, *Politics* 1289 b 38: *EGA* 163ff, 256 notes 21–2
22 *EGA* 159ff and pl. 2 (Nestor); but see J. K. Anderson's discussion, *AJA* 1965, 349–53

CHAPTER III

1 Miss Lorimer's fundamental article in *BSA* 1947, 76–138 now stands in need of some modification; see *e.g. EGA* 89, 138, 197–9
2 *EGA* 9, 13ff
3 *EGA* 10, 20ff
4 For a very early example, see *Ol. ber.* I, pl. 52
5 ffoulkes (Ch. I, note 25) 96: Persson (Ch. I note 26), 119

6 Figurine, *AJA* 1944, 1–4: Italian barbute, R. E. Oakeshott, *The Archaeology of Weapons* (1960), 291, pl. 14 c

7 For Insular and 'Illyrian' helmets, see *EGA* 16–20, with references

8 See the fine examples in *Ol. ber.* II, pls. 40–2, III, pls. 47–51: *EGA* 88

9 *EGA* 61–7; a second *antilabē* is sometimes seen at the left-hand edge, perhaps an emergency spare

10 Archilochus fr. 6: Alcaeus, in Herodotus V, 95, 1–2: Anacreon fr. 51 (Diehl): *cf.* Horace, *Odes* II, 7, 10

11 On shield-bands, E. Kunze, *Ol. Forsch.* II, especially 215ff on Argos, and the catalogue, 251–6: blazons, *e.g. Ol. ber.* I, pls. 11–13, II, pls. 23–6, V, pls. 28–33

12 *HM* 161ff

13 On *mitrai*, *HM* 247ff and D. Levi, *Annuario della Scuola archeologica di Atene* 1930–1, 43ff; Brandenburg, *Studien zur Mitra* (1966)

14 For discussions of this, see *JdI* 1938, 104ff, *BSA* 1947, 107ff and *EGA* 84

15 Argos grave, *EGA* 124, pl. 35: representations, *ibid.* pls. 15, 33, 36 and *BSA* 1947, 81ff, figs. 2–3, 8–10

16 Sword-combats, *Corpus Vasorum Antiquorum*, Berlin I, pls. 28, 1; 44, 2; *BSA* 1934–5, pl. 52 a: one-edged types, *e.g.* J. K. Brock, *Fortetsa* (1957), pl. 75, 1085, and H. G. G. Payne, *Necrocorinthia* (1931), 126, fig. 44 *bis*

17 *EGA* pl. 36

18 Aristotle, *Constitution of Athenians* XLII, 4

19 Aristotle, *Politics* 1289 b, 39; the best discussion is A. Andrewes, *The Greek Tyrants* (1956), 31–8

20 Relief, *Fortetsa* (note 16), pls. 115, 168: miniature armour, *e.g. BSA* 1939–40, 54ff: helmets, corslets and greaves, *EGA* 28ff, 74ff, 87ff

21 Callinus, fr. 1: Alcaeus, fr. 54, *EGA* 182–3: actual armour, C. Blinkenberg, *Lindos* I (1931), 186–92, pls. 22–5; most of the Samos finds await detailed publication, but for helmeted head see *AM* 1957, Beilage 62, 1

22 Herodotus II, 152: Ephorus fr. 12 (Jacoby): Diodorus I, 66: see *JHS* 1964, 117ff for a discussion

23 On the Ionian helmet, *EGA* 31–4: frieze from Pazarli, Phrygia, E. Akurgal, *Phrygische Kunst* (1955), pls. 46–9: Cyprus bowl, *JHS* 1933, pl. 3: Corinthian helmet in Cyprus, *AR* 1955, 43

24 On Tyrtaeus see M. P. Nilsson, *Klio* 1929, 241–4: *BSA* 1947, 121ff: *EGA* 181ff

25 See R. M. Dawkins *et al.*, *Artemis Orthia* (1929), pls. 183, 191: on dating, J. Boardman, *BSA* 1963, 1–7: later blazons, Eupolis, fr. 359; Theopompus, fr. 91 (Kock); Bacchylides, fr. 21 (Snell); Xenophon, *Hellenica* IV, 4, 10 and VII, 5, 20

26 Shield-bands, above note 11: helmet-rims, *Ol. ber.* VII, 91ff

27 *BCH* 1944–5, 54, fig. 15 and *EGA* pl. 14: still-life scenes, *e.g. EGA* pl. 33; *cf. JdI* 1938, 105, fig. 8; trumpet-signals, *e.g.* Thucydides VI, 69; Xenophon *Anabasis* IV, 4, 22; see J. K. Anderson, *JHS* 1965, 1–4

28 Corinthian hoplite scenes, *BSA* 1947, 81ff, figs. 2-3, 7-10: pipers at Sparta, *e.g.* Thucydides V, 70 and Polybius IV, 20, 6: hoplite armies, Herodotus IX, 28, 3-6; Thucydides I, 49 and III, 105 (Ambracia)

29 Protoattic vases, see *BSA* 1947, 86ff, figs. 4, 6: Athenian corslets, Aelian *Var. Hist.* III, 24 and Pollux, *Onomasticon* I, 149: equipping Argives, Thucydides VIII, 25, 1. On the Attic helmet, see especially J. D. Beazley, *Development of Attic Black-figure* (1951), 89 ff: *PCG* pls. 4, 31-2 and 5, 35-6: *AGA* 13, etc., but the type of helmet worn by Amazons is often irregular in detail: *cf. SSG*, fig. 84 for normal use. A surviving example is in the British Museum, *GRL* fig. 68, no. 224

30 On 'Chalcidian' helmet, see *EGA* 34, 222 note 118: vase in Berlin, A. Rumpf, *Chalkidische Vasen* (1927), pl. 121: the type is worn by Athena in copies of Myron's Marsyas group (*SSG* figs. 589-90): red-figure portrayals include that of the left-hand figure in the well-known cup by the Penthesilea painter, *HGVP* pl. 168. See further *AD* 1964, 85-9

31 *Archaeology* 1952, 40-6

32 On Euboea, J. Boardman, *BSA* 1957, 27ff: *EGA* 202, 265, notes 44-5: Geometric vase, *BSA* 1952, pl. 3A, and J. M. Davison, *Attic Geometric Workshops* (1961), 67-73

33 Homer, *Iliad* II, 543-4: Archilochus fr. 3, 4-5: Anth. Pal. XIV, 73: chariot-procession, Strabo X, 447

34 Tegea, Orchomenos, Mantinea, Herodotus I, 66-7 and VII, 202: shield-bands, see note 11: greaves, *AE* 1904, 207, fig. 25 and *AR* 1959-60, 11: Bassae miniatures, *AE* 1910, 311, figs. 30, 33

35 Xenophon, *Hellenica* VII, 4, 30 (*cf.* VI, 5, 19); Polybius IV, 74, 6

36 *AD* 1961-2, 128ff, pls. 156, 153 a

37 *AE* 1927-8, 107, fig. 66: compare *BCH* 1959, 695, fig. 9 from Macedonia

38 Tanagraian shields, *Ol. ber.* II 69 and V 37: Archilochus, fr. 6: Naxos, Herodotus V, 30, 6: Siphnos, *BSA* 1949, 38ff: Ithaca, *BSA* 1953, 340: Leukas, Kephallenia, Herodotus IX, 28, 5: Zakynthos, Thucydides I, 47: Aetolia, *e.g.* Thucydides III, 96-8; *Ol. Forsch.* II, 252. Note too the panoply-reliefs from the islands, like *JdI* 1913, pl. 26; *AR* 1962-3, fig. 31

39 Dedications, *Ol.* V (1896), 373ff, nos. 254-6, *Ol. ber.* III, 78-9 and V, 37-40: Corinthian helmets (two-piece), see *Ol. ber.* VI, 132 and VII, 66

40 Etruria and Rome: for a fuller discussion, see *JHS* 1965, 110-22: for lists of finds, *EGA* 232 note 105, 239, note 53: there are corslets of later form from Italy in Florence (from Orvieto—G. Dennis, *Cities and Cemeteries of Etruria* II (1883), 103), in Hamburg, Karlsruhe (from Vulci), Munich and London (from Ruvo and elsewhere, H. B. Walters, *Catalogue of the Bronzes in the British Museum* (1899), nos. 2846ff); one in the John Woodman Higgins Armory, Worcester, Mass., (S. V. Grancsay, *Catalogue of Armor* (1961), 21, no. 1132) may be from Italy: Agathocles, Diodorus XX, 11, 1; XXI, 3

41 Corslets: *EGA* 77ff, referring to G. von Merhart in *Origines* (Como, 1954),

33ff. 'Illyrian' helmets, *e.g. Ol. ber.* VI, 135ff, notes 22–7 and 144, notes 45–6, and *Dacia* 1958, 437f: corslets in Bulgaria, L. Ognenova, *BCH* 1961, 501–38: helmets in Spain, A. Garcia y Bellido, *Hispania Graeca* II (1948), 82, 84, pls. 19 and 22

42 Persepolis, J. Boardman, *The Greeks Overseas* (1964), 124: Carchemish, C. L. Woolley, *Carchemish* II (1921), 81, 128, pls. 24, 25 a: Alcaeus fr. 50 (Diehl)

43 Aristotle fr. 498 (Rose), *cf.* Xenophon, *Memorabilia* III, 9, 2: Phrynichus, in Bekker, *Anecdota Graeca* I, 33, 25: Amazons, *AGA passim* and, for vases inspired by lost wall-paintings, 161ff, nos. 2, 6, and 7 especially (pls. LXXIV–LXXV): odd-shaped *peltai*, Dionysius II, 70; Suidas, s.v.; Pollux I, 133 who, quoting Xenophon *Anabasis* V, 4, 12, identifies *pelta* with *gerrhon*

44 Aristotle, *Constitution of Athenians* XV, 2

45 On bronze-faced shields, see especially E. Kunze, *Kretische Bronzereliefs* (1930): Lydos painting, *AGA* 14, p . XVII, 1

46 Throwing-loops, see especially *Acta Archaeologica* (Copenhagen) 1960, 130, fig. 5: *EGA* pls. 33, 36 and, on javelins generally, 137ff.

47 On spear-butts, see *Ol. Forsch.* I, 154–8, pls. 63–8: carried by peltast, *e.g.* Daremberg and Saglio, *Dictionnaire des Antiquités* I (s.v. 'clipeus'), fig. 1664: clubs, Herodotus I, 59, 6 and Aristotle, *Politics* 1311 b 26

48 References to bow, *e.g.* Sophocles, *Ajax* 1120–2; Aristophanes, fr. 411; Plutarch, *Moralia* 234 E: Cretan bow, *HM* 278ff, pls. XXI, 1 and XXIII, 1: arrow, *EGA* 144–8: Mercenaries, Pausanias IV, 8, 3; 10, 1; 19, 4: Thucydides VI, 43; VII, 57, etc.: on the range of Greek bows, W. E. McLeod, *Phoenix* 1965, 1ff. I am most grateful to Mr D. J. F. Hill for references and information on ancient archery, used here and elsewhere

49 Smyrna, *BSA* 1958–9, 128ff: C. Blinkenberg, *Lindos* I (1931), 194ff: for other references, *EGA* 250ff, notes 25, 40, 42, 45, 47

50 On the Scythian bow, *HM* 285ff, 302ff, fig. 37, 2; but *n.b. EGA* 142–3. Excellent illustrations of the bow in its various states are *HM* pls. XXII, 1 and 4; XXIII, 2; XXXI, 2

51 The best recent study of Scythian arrowheads is T. Sulimirski's in *Artibus Asiae* 1954, 282ff: see *EGA* 148ff for additions and minor modifications

52 Scythian bow, see note 50 and add Beazley, *Development of Attic Black-figure*, pl. 3, lower

53 On this subject, see the excellent work of M. F. Vos, *Scythian Archers in Archaic Attic Vase-painting* (Groningen, 1963), which revises some long-held opinions

54 Sling-bullets, see especially D. M. Robinson, *Excavations at Olynthus* X (1941), 418ff: representations, Ecole française d'Athènes, *Délos* X (1928), 137, fig. 3 and R. M. Dawkins, *Artemis Orthia*, pls. 15–16

55 Good illustrations of this type of weapon are *GRL* fig. 94 a–b and *AE*

1927–8, 107, fig. 66. Vos (above, note 53) shows an example of the Scythian axe (pl. 16)

56 On the Athenian 'Knights', see W. Helbig's writings, *Mémoires de l'Academie des Inscriptions et Belles-Lettres* 1902, 157ff and *Sitzungsberichte der Bayerischen Akademie der Wissenschaften* 1911, 37ff: Mantinea, Thucydides V, 72: on horses and breeding, J. K. Anderson, *Ancient Greek Horsemanship* (1961), 16ff, 36ff, and G. Devereux, *Classical Quarterly* 1965, 176–84

57 Plutarch, *Moralia* 760–1: Herodotus V, 63, 3, etc., and VII, 196

58 On bits, see Anderson, *op. cit.* (note 56), 73–5, pl. 33: blinkers and forehead-guards, *EGA* 33ff, 164ff, with references

59 Herodotus VII, 158: Diodorus XI, 21ff on Himera: chamfreins, *EGA* 165, 258 note 32

60 Lydia, Sappho fr. 27 (Diehl), 16 (Lobel and Page), line 19: Cyprus, Herodotus V, 113, 1: Cyrene, *e.g.* Pindar, *Pythian* IV, 7; Aeneas Tacticus XVI, 14; Diodorus XVIII, 19, 4 and XX, 41, 1: dogs, R. M. Cook in *Festschrift für Andreas Rumpf* (1952), 38ff

CHAPTER IV

1 Amasis, Herodotus II, 182 and III, 47, 2: Assyrians, IX, 63

2 Among the Archaic monuments which show it are the Aristion stele and the crouching archer from the East pediment of the Temple of Aphaea, *SSG* figs. 389, 424: worn by Achilles, *HGVP* pls. 188 and XL (the scales at the sides are faintly visible): but it is regular on red-figure battle-scenes from Oltos onwards, *e.g. AGA* pl. LXVIII, 4; *HGVP* pls. 114–15, 125, etc.; and the arming-scene by Euthymides, E. Pfuhl, *Malerei und Zeichnung* (1923), figs. 364–5

3 Scales from Olympia and Delphi, *EGA* 85 and note 42: there are some representations which show *all*-scale corslets with shoulder-pieces, *e.g. HGVP* pls. 118, 130: bronze finials, *e.g. Ol. Forsch.* II, Beilage 9, 2, from Dodona

4 Aristion, see note 2: Marathon, Herodotus VI, 112, 1, but see *JHS* 1964, 126 for doubts about the distance: Olympia, Pausanias V, 8, 10

5 Good portrayals of the new type are *HGVP* pls. 144 (top), 178–9: finds in Italy, see above, Ch. III, note 40

6 Greaves, see Ch. III, note 8: ankle-guards, *Ol. ber.* II, pl. 43, III, f. 102 and *EGA* 240–1, note 55: arm-guards, etc., Beazley, *Etruscan Vase-painting* (1947), 136ff, 301; *AM* 1916, 367; *EGA* 240, note 54

7 On earlier models, E. Kunze in *Ol. ber.* VII, 77–128: good examples of the latest form are *Ol. ber.* III, pls. 44–5, V, pls. 34–9; *GRL* fig. 63, no. 210; and in art, *HGVP* pls. 114–15, 125: portrait-heads, *e.g.* copies of Kresilas' Pericles, *SSG* fig. 624: South Italy, see p. 128: Aristion, see note 2—it is possible that he originally wore a different form of helmet (even perhaps a

Corinthian one tilted back) and that, after damage to the stone, this was trimmed off

8 Boeotian reliefs, e.g. BCH 1902, pls. VII–VIII; P. M. Fraser and T. Rönne, Boeotian and West Greek Tombstones (1957), 66–8, pls. 1, 18; A. Rumpf, Kranos Boiotourges (Abhandlungen der Preussischen Akademie der Wissenschaften, Philosophisch-historische Klasse, 1943, no. 8): earlier version, e.g. AGA pl. LXXIV, 4: compare Polynices' hat on a pelikē, R. M. Cook, Greek Painted Pottery (1960) pl. 45

9 On Thracian helmets, see B. Schroeder in JdI 1912, 317–44: the best early portrayal is HGVP pls. 176, 178: 'Illyrian' helmet, e.g. Pfuhl, op. cit. (see note 2), fig. 504, left; JdI 1912, 339, fig. 17

10 For the cord, see GRL fig. 93; AGA pl. LXXI, 3; HGVP pls. 144, 174, 179, with a different and earlier arrangement on pl. 139: studs, e.g. Ol. ber. II, 91, fig. 10: blazons, see C. Seltman, Athens, its History and Coinage (1924), passim, and the criticisms of L. Lacroix, Etudes d'Archéologie Classique 1955–6, 89ff

11 Finds of blazons, see Ch. III, note 11: apron, e.g. HGVP pl. 139, top (visible below diagonal crack) and, better, 179

12 On material, EGA 134: Italian spearheads, Ol. Forsch. I, pls. 56–7: hoplites with two spears, e.g. Vos (see Ch. III, note 53) pls. 6 b, 8: Plato, Euthydemus 299 C: Euripides, Hercules Furens 193–4

13 For portrayals, HGVP pls. 170–1 and 179, lower left: similar blows could be struck with the older two-edged sword, ibid. pls. 114, 178: actual examples, e.g. GRL fig. 94 c and Archaeologia 1912–13, pl. XIII: on Harmodius, see B. B. Shefton, AJA 1960, 173–9

14 Ctesias, Persica XXVI: Salamis, Plutarch, Themistocles XIV, 1; Aeschylus, Persae 460; mounted bowmen, Thucydides II, 13, 8 (cf. V, 84, 1; VI, 94, 4, etc.): Sphacteria, IV, 28 and following chapters: Spartan reaction, IV, 55, 2: Sicilian expedition, especially VI, 43, 1: Gelon, Herodotus VII, 158

15 Marathon, see especially E. J. Forsdyke in Proceedings of the Society of Antiquaries 1919–20, 152ff: Thermopylae, AA 1940, 200, fig. 47: Acropolis, Hesperia 1935, 114, fig. 4

16 For Olympia finds, see Ol. V, 359ff, nos. 245ff: Hieron's trophy also Ol. IV, 172 (its inscription is now closely paralleled on a newly-found Corinthian helmet, BCH 1960, 721, fig. 12): other dedications, Ol. ber. II, 68–9; V, 37–40 and 69–74 (Miltiades): BCH 1960, 716, fig. 4: AE 1925–6, 87ff: AD 1916, 88, 114, o. 80: Syracuse, Ol. ber. V, 38

17 These vases are shown by Anne Bovon, BCH 1963, 579–602: Nike temple relief, SSG fig. 295

18 Apron, e.g. HGVP pls. 139, top (visible below diagonal crack) and, better, 179: Alcaeus, fr. 54 (Diehl), line 5: European greaves e.g. EGA 86: cavalry numbers in Athens, e.g. Thucydides II, 13, 7 and Demosthenes XIV, 13: bit, Anderson, op. cit. (Ch. III, note 56), 70–1, pl. 35; cf. 36 b

19 *AE* 1937, I, 140ff

20 On mercenaries, H. W. Parke, *Greek Mercenary Soldiers* (1933) and G. T. Griffith, *MHW* are equally valuable for their respective periods: on Sicily, Polyaenus V, 6 and Diodorus XI, 72, 3

21 See *Hesperia* 1956, 307ff: pay-rates, *MHW* 294–5: Aristophanes *Peace* 1210ff

22 Anderson, *op. cit.* (Ch. III, note 56), chapter XII, is very valuable on the whole of Xenophon's treatise, of which he gives a translation: see his article, *JHS* 1960, 7–8 on *parapleuridia:* for cavalry-corslet in Xenophon, *cf. Anabasis* III, 4, 48: for illustration of *cheir*, Kromayer fig. 38: on Xenophon's pessimism, compare his *Cavalry Commander* I, 17, 18: on the cavalry-stelai, K. Friis Johansen, *The Attic Grave-reliefs* (Copenhagen, 1951), 48ff and *SSG* fig. 215

23 Thrasyllus, Xenophon *Hellenica* 1, 2, 1: *Inscriptiones Graecae* I₂ 97. 17; 99. 5

24 Plutarch, *Moralia* 596 D: Pollux I, 134: Aelian, *Tactica* XVI, 3

25 Xenophon, *Hellenica* VII, 1, 21

26 Plutarch, *Timoleon* XXV, 2; XXVII, 2–3; Diodorus XVI, 80, 6

CHAPTER V

1 On this whole field, W. W. Tarn, *Hellenistic Military and Naval Developments* (1930), M. Launey, *Recherches sur les Armées Hellénistiques* (1949–50), and G. T. Griffith's article in *Proceedings of the Cambridge Philological Society* 1956–7, 3–10 are very useful. Macedonian graves include a number interspersed with the Early Iron Age tumuli at Verghina, described in *AD* 1961–2, 218–88 (with a possible *sarissa*-head in pl. 146 a, top right), and 1963, 217–32

2 Kromayer 98ff, especially 108–10 and 133–5, is valuable on hypaspists and other troops, with their equipment; see also J. R. Hamilton in *Classical Quarterly* 1955, 218–19, answered in Griffith's article (note 1)

3 Earlier Macedonian coins, *e.g. JdI* 1912, 341, fig. 18, 12–13: Thracian helmets, *ibid.* 317ff: 'Chalcidian', *BSA* 1918–19, pls. 8, 1 and 1: Seleucus, *PCG* pl. 27, 11

4 Olympia battering-ram, *Ol. ber.* V, 75f.: catapults, Tarn, *op. cit.* (note 1), 101ff. Olynthus, D. M. Robinson, *Excavations at Olynthus* X (1941), 378–446, especially 382ff (large 'arrowheads') and 392ff (Cypriot form)

5 See Kromayer 110ff on shields and other equipment: Griffith's article (note 1) on corslets and much else: Thracian helmets, see note 3

6 The best summary is F. Lammert's article in Pauly-Wissowa, *Realencyclopädie der klassischen Alterthumswissenschaft*, zweite Reihe, I A 2 (1920), 2315–30 ('sarissa')

7 The *rhomphaia* should be a cutting weapon—a sword or more probably a kind of halberd—since it is hung from the right shoulder (Plutarch, *Aemilius* XVIII 3: see A. J. Reinach in *BCH* 1910, 444ff): but in Latin contexts it

is usually explained as a missile: on the impact of the Spanish sword, Livy XXXI, 34: Pella mosaic, M. Robertson, *Greek Painting* (Geneva, 1959), 166–9

8 Coins, *e.g.* Kromayer fig. 32: Issus mosaic, M. Grant (ed.) *The Birth of Western Civilization*, 65: Granicus and Gaugamela, Diodorus XVII, 20; Plutarch, *Alexander* XVI, 5 and XXXII, 5 and 8: Malli, Arrian, *Anabasis* VI, 10, 1 and Plutarch, *Alexander* LXIII, 3: Persian cavalry-armour, *e.g.* Arrian II, 11, 3 and Plutarch, *Alexander* XVI, 4: on Alexander's cavalry, P. A. Brunt, *JHS* 1963, 27–46

9 See Asclepiodotus IV, 1 and 3: for doubts about this, Veith in Kromayer 358

10 Griffith, *MHW* 122–3, believes that he in effect counted the 'Egyptian phalanx' of 20,000 twice

11 Pergamon shield, *Alterthümer von Pergamon* X, 33, pl. 27: Pydna monument, *BCH* 1910, 433ff, and compare the Boscoreale painting, *JdI* 1923–4, pl. II: other reliefs Kromayer figs. 33, 35–6, and compare Anderson, *op. cit.* (Ch. III, note 56), pl. 13 a: Monunios helmet, *JdI* 1912, 327, Beilage 12, 6: the helmet referred to as a *kōnos* in inscriptions from Amphipolis and Delos (see *Revue Archéologique* 1935, II, 31, line 4 and 37, note 2) will be of either Thracian or, more probably, Boeotian type.

12 Griffith, *MHW* 119, 319

13 Cestrosphendonē, Polybius XXVII, 9 and Livy XLII, 65, 9: pole-sling, Kromayer 234, fig. 70: Cretan arrowheads, *British Museum Quarterly* 1951–2, 45ff and *EGA* 147 (I owe my knowledge of the British example to Mr. Ll. R. Laing): Magnesia, Livy XXXVII, 40: Cretans as shield-bearers, Polybius X, 29, 6 and 30, 9 (Livy, XLII, 55, 10, speaks of a 'Creticus armatus' but this certainly does not imply body-armour)

14 Inscription, W. Dittenberger, *Sylloge Inscriptionum Graecarum* (1915), I, 421, lines 40ff: Boeotian helmets, see *e.g.* the stele in *BCH* 1880, pl. VII and the 'Alexander' sarcophagus, *AA* 1894, 21, figs. 16–17: for later modifications, *e.g. PCG* pls. 40, 23 and 41, 26 and 32: Tigris helmet, Anderson, *op. cit.* (Ch. III, note 56) 148: Lindos, C. Blinkenberg (ed.), *Die Lindische Tempel-chronik* (Lietzmanns kleine Texte, no. 131): Dodona, C. Carapanos, *Dodone et ses Ruines* (1878), especially pls 55–6: light-armed Greek troops, Kromayer 137 with references: peltastēs on the stage, Parke, *op. cit.* (Ch. IV, note 20), 234

15 Athenian inscriptions, *Inscriptiones Graecae* II₂ 120.37; *cf.* 1649.14; 665.28–9: Launey, *op. cit.* (note 1), II, 826ff: Ceos, *Inscriptiones Graecae* XII, 5, 647: Olbia, E. H. Minns, *Scythians and Greeks* (1913), 66 note 10, 465

16 Plutarch, *Cleomenes* XI: on Boeotia and Achaea, see M. Feyel, *Polybe et l'historie de la Béotie* (1942), 213ff and Launey, *op. cit.* (note 1) I, 151, 361–2

17 Philopoemen's reform may not have lasted: *cf.* Livy XLII, 55, 10, after his death: Polybius XVIII, 18, 3

18 On South Italian armament, see F. Weege in *JdI* 1909, 141–58: Paestan painting and Italiote vases, A. D. Trendall, *Paestan Pottery* (1936), 89–91, pls. 31 b–c and A. Maiuri, *Roman Painting* (Geneva, 1953), 16: late Corinthian helmets, *e.g. GRL* fig. 64, no. 213: Tarantinoi, Griffith, *MHW* 246–51 and Kromayer 139

19 Plutarch, *Aemilius* XIX, 1

20 Plutarch, *Sulla* XVIII, 4; XIX, 2: contrast *Lucullus* VII, 4

21 Griffith, *MHW* 322, note 2

INDEX